Aristotle's
Metaphysics

CONTINUUM READER'S GUIDES

Continuum Reader's Guides are clear, concise, and accessible introductions to key texts in literature and philosophy. Each book explores the themes, context, criticism, and influence of key works, providing a practical introduction to close reading, guiding students towards a thorough understanding of the text. They provide an essential, up-to-date resource, ideal for undergraduate students.

Reader's Guides available from Continuum:

A READER'S GUIDE

Aristotle's *Metaphysics*

EDWARD C. HALPER

continuum

Continuum International Publishing Group

The Tower Building	80 Maiden Lane
11 York Road	Suite 704
London	New York
SE1 7NX	NY 10038

www.continuumbooks.com

British Library Cataloguing-in-Publication Data
A catalogue record for this book is available from the British Library.

ISBN: HB: 978-1-4411-3191-1
PB: 978-1-4411-0713-8

Library of Congress Cataloging-in-Publication Data
Halper, Edward C., 1951-
Aristotle's "Metaphysics" : a reader's guide / Edward Halper.
pages cm. – (Reader's guides)
Includes bibliographical references and index.
ISBN 978-1-4411-0713-8 (pbk. : alk. paper)– ISBN 978-1-4411-3191-1
(hardcover : alk. paper)– ISBN 978-1-4411-9275-2 (ebook epub : alk. paper)–
ISBN 978-1-4411-1773-1 (ebook pdf : alk. paper) 1. Aristotle. Metaphysics. I. Title.
B434.H34 2012
110–dc23
2011049276

Typeset by Fakenham Prepress Solutions, Fakenham, Norfolk NR21 8NN
Printed and bound in India

CONTENTS

PREFACE

No work of philosophy is more important than Aristotle's *Metaphysics*. No work of philosophy is more difficult for both beginners and experienced philosophers. The difficulties are worth confronting because Aristotle poses and answers questions at the heart of philosophy: what is it to be? what is the nature of reality? what is the first principle of all things? what is the relation between philosophy and other branches of knowledge? Aristotle's answers may not be widely accepted; they may not be right; but they are always interesting and always important windows on the work of later philosophers.

The aim of this book is to help you read the *Metaphysics* and, more importantly, wrestle with the issues it addresses. Every page of Aristotle's text, indeed virtually every line is controversial. The writing style is terse and often crabbed. The text rarely provides those signposts and summaries that orient the reader by letting him or her know how an argument contributes to the work as a whole or how much of a task has been accomplished and what remains. The arguments are often very abbreviated, with important assumptions omitted and without much context. For centuries readers relied on Greek and, then, Latin line-by-line commentaries to explain how to read the text. But these works are not without their own prejudices, and in the last century scholars have set them aside to explore the text directly, bit by bit. As a result, the literature on the *Metaphysics* is often piecemeal and unhelpful for the student struggling to understand what the issues are. In contrast, I have tried here to provide the reader with a sense of the issues and the way Aristotle formulates and resolves them. The account sketched here is elaborated and defended in my three-volume: *One and Many in Aristotle's Metaphysics*, published by Parmenides Press. My interpretation has hardly stilled controversy. But a student needs a certain familiarity with the issues to appreciate the controversy. That is what I have tried to do here, namely, to give readers a reference point, a sense of what is at issue along with a coherent way of looking at the text. These are preliminary to any serious treatment of textual controversies. Again, this book does not offer a definitive resolution of the issues so much as a beginning from which they can be appreciated. Ideally, the reader will be led to reflect on the text herself and to engage the philosophical issues that Aristotle addresses.

The standard Oxford translation of the *Metaphysics* was made by W. D. Ross in the early twentieth century. It was revised by Jonathan Barnes and appears as part of the two-volume *The Complete Works of Aristotle* (Princeton University Press). It reads well, but Ross does not translate key terms consistently. A number of other translations have appeared since, and each has its advantages. I like Hippocrates Apostle's translation, and it is more consistent. Richard Hope includes an analytical index that allows the reader to see which Greek term is being translated. Hugh Lawson-Tancred manages a rather colloquial translation and includes a lengthy introduction and summaries before each chapter. Joe Sachs takes a rather different approach: he avoids using the standard vocabulary, derived from Latin, that is widely used to translate Aristotle's text. Instead, he renders Aristotle's technical terms into ordinary English, though he sometimes resorts to constructing his own terms and phrases, as does Aristotle himself. There is much to be said for Sachs's approach. The standard vocabulary has made its way into English to such an extent that the reader often imagines that he understands the meaning of terms that Aristotle uses in ways quite different from their current, ordinary usage. Sachs's translation is nicely concrete, and it forces the reader to reckon with the text. However, it also requires a good deal more patience than the others. Although I myself often use it in my own courses, it has not found widespread acceptance. Its virtue is also its vice: because Sachs uses ordinary English terms, the reader can easily miss the technical vocabulary at work in a passage. Since one task of this book is to explain this vocabulary, I have decided, reluctantly, to use Barnes's revision of Ross's translation in textual quotations. Those using most other translations should be able to find their way through these quotations. Many translations print the page and line number from Bekker's critical edition of Aristotle's work (orginally published in 1831) making it possible for those who cannot read the work in the original to compare translations. Bekker's text appeared in large folio pages with two columns. Hence, a reference to 980a1 designates the first line of the first column on page 980. Bekker notes different manuscript readings at the bottom of his page. Since some passages have many readings and others fewer, the amount of text is not the same on every page.

It is customary to refer to books of the *Metaphysics* by the Greek letters that number them. One reason is that there are two introductory books and some scholars deny that the second of them is authentic. Since the numbering of subsequent books depends on whether the second is included, using Greek letters for all the books avoids ambiguity. The two introductory books are designated with upper and lower case alphas: A and α. I have used Roman numerals to designate books of other Aristotelian works.

It is sometimes said that "meta" in "metaphysics" means "after" rather than "beyond" and that the work gets its name from its location on the editor's shelf, as it were, "after" the *Physics*. The corollary of this thought is that the books that we group together do not have any intrinsic unity or internal coherence. This is a conclusion that some scholars have reached after considering the text carefully and finding unavoidable contradictions. As I said, this is not the place to consider scholarly claims, but I have tried to show here how the *Metaphysics* can be read consistently. Indeed, the account I present here shows it to be a carefully crafted work that *does* aim at causes "beyond" physical nature. Before the reader can judge between these conclusions or, better, draw her own, she needs to look carefully at the text as it has come down to us, for this text is the datum from which all claims about the order and coherence of the *Metaphysics* begin.

This book is written to help students learn to read the text of Aristotle's *Metaphysics*. It cannot serve as a substitute for that text. A good course in the *Metaphysics* or any other great philosophical work is not primarily about grasping a set of philosophical positions. There are, of course, Aristotelian doctrines to be learned and appreciated. However, what should be center stage are the problems that are at issue. Aristotle spends an entire book (book B) setting out the problems of metaphysics, and at every turn he seems to raise still others. The best way to come to understand Aristotle's text is to appreciate the force of these problems. They are not just

Aristotle's problems. They are problems likely to be encountered by anyone who tries to think seriously about metaphysics. Generally, once one appreciates the force of the problems, Aristotle's solutions become intelligible and plausible. As an exercise, it is helpful to try to think of alternative solutions and to reflect on why Aristotle did not adopt these solutions.

The problems Aristotle wrestles with in the *Metaphysics* and the solutions he advances are deep and far reaching. The usual picture of Aristotle's philosophy as close to common sense and ordinary language does not do the *Metaphysics* justice, for these are not ordinary problems and they are not resolved by appeals to common sense. Instead, Aristotle introduces new approaches to problems and new doctrines that, as Aristotle himself acknowledges, remain challenging, no matter how familiar one becomes with them. My brief presentation of these doctrines cannot address all the objections that readers will raise. But this limitation is an advantage if the reader will take the opportunity to reflect further on her objections and to seek out Aristotle's answers.

One does not come to understand this or any other philosophical text by memorizing its contents. Instead, the reader must be prepared to question the text, to challenge it, to consider alternative positions, to formulate his own arguments against the text's arguments and positions, and also to consider how Aristotle might respond to these counter arguments. All this can be called "engaging the text." To help facilitate the first steps of this process, the bulk of this book works through Aristotle's text section by section with the aim of expounding the issues it addresses, the way it addresses them, and the solutions Aristotle advances. Many sections conclude the exposition of the text with questions for reflection. These questions are difficult to answer. Good philosophical questions do not have easy answers, and a profound and important work like the *Metaphysics* is best approached with questions.

CHAPTER ONE

Context

There are two bits of intellectual context that are essential for understanding the *Metaphysics*. The first is the tradition of metaphysical investigation among earlier Greek philosophers, that is, the philosophers who are called the "Presocratics" because they lived before or at the same time as Socrates, and Aristotle's teacher, Plato. The second is Aristotle's own idea of a science, for he, like other Greek thinkers, regards metaphysics as a science.

First, though, let me make some general observations about Greek notions of science and metaphysics. Our word "science" comes from the Latin *scientia*, which is itself a translation of the Greek *epistēmē*. The latter can also be translated directly into English as "knowledge." In other words, the same Greek term can be translated as "science" or as "[branch of] knowledge": *any* branch of knowledge is called a "science." Moreover, an art (*technē*), such as housebuilding, also counts as a branch of knowledge and, thus, as a science. It can be disorienting for contemporary readers to hear about a "science of metaphysics" or a "science of ethics," but the term "science" should help to remind us that Aristotle assumes that knowledge must have a characteristic organization and structure. Both Plato and Aristotle distinguish branches of knowledge from each other by (1) their subject matters and (2) their principles. Physics, mathematics, ethics, and house-building all have different subject matters. The principles of these subject matters can be: (a) that within the subject matter in respect of which all else in the subject matter exists or is known (as the unit is the principle of number because all the counting numbers are composed of units), (b) those feelings, habits, and goals that motivate action (as happiness is a principle because it is the goal of all actions), and (c) the product the craftsman produces (as the finished house is a principle of the housebuilder because it determines the steps she needs to take to produce it).

It was Aristotle's editor who gave the name "metaphysics" to the science he calls "wisdom," "first philosophy," and "the science of being as being." Other Greek thinkers did not use any of these names, except perhaps "wisdom," but they all had the concept of a branch of knowledge that differs from others because it seeks to know the first principles of all things. That is to say, its subject matter is all things, and its principles are that in respect of which *all* things are and are known. Plato thinks of it as the ruling science because it both rules the other sciences and fits a person to be a political ruler. Aristotle distinguishes the highest theoretical science, metaphysics, from the highest practical science, politics. It is not obvious that there are first principles and highest causes. Metaphysics must discover *whether* they exist and, if so, *what* they are. If there were no first principles, there would not be a science of metaphysics. Thus, in investigating whether there are first principles, metaphysics is investigating its own existence.

Greek philosophers assume that a cause is some sort of thing. This contrasts with modern thought where a cause is usually a law. Aristotle offers a famous account of the different sorts of causes, as we will see, in *Metaphysics* A.3. All causes are principles, but some principles are not causes. Some readers take these latter principles to be laws, but Aristotle thinks they, too, must either be some sort of entity or somehow linked with an entity. Greek philosophers have no place for a principle that, like our principle of conservation of energy (energy is neither created nor destroyed), is a principle of everything without itself being anything.

Earlier Greek metaphysics

For Aristotle's philosophical predecessors, the central metaphysical issue is the problem of the one and the many: are all things one or are they many? We can appreciate one version of this problem from modern physics, where it is posed as follows: are all things composed of many distinct elementary particles or are what appear to be distinct particles rather different states of a single entity? At one point, electrons, protons, and neutrons were thought to be the most elementary particles, but most physicists today think these are composed of still more fundamental constituents. Some claim that all these constituent particles are simply forms of energy and that, therefore, all is one. Analogously, ancient thinkers ask whether earth, air, fire, and water are distinct and irreducible elements of all things or whether all these are merely different forms of the same element, say, water. In either case, it is assumed that, by itself, *each* element is one and that, by being one, it is prior to any plurality formed from multiple elements.

There is another way that all might be one. Suppose that there is a single character that belongs to every being. (Such a character is called a "universal," a "one [character] over many [things]"; a genus is an example of a universal because it belongs to each of its instances.) Then, everything that *is* would have the character, and everything that *is not* would not have it. All that is would, thus, have the same character, a character that would signify what it is to be, that is, the nature of being. A surprising consequence of this line of thought is that there would be no motion, for a motion occurs when something that is not comes to be, but whatever has the nature of being *already* is, and whatever lacks this nature and thereby is not, is nothing. It makes no sense to speak of nothing's acquiring the nature of being or, indeed, acquiring any other nature. Furthermore, if there were a nature that were common to all beings, everything that is would have this nature and all would be one. This is the reasoning of Parmenides. Greek thinkers took these arguments to be so powerful that, after Parmenides, the central metaphysical issue was how there could be a plurality or a motion.

The ancient atomists are among those who offer an answer. They propose that there are indivisible bits of matter, atoms. Being consists of these atoms; not-being is the void. These philosophers concede that being does not change because individual atoms cannot alter their natures. However, motion and plurality are possible because groups of atoms do alter their positions relative to each other.

Plato and his school, the Academy, have a different response to Parmenides. Although there are some indications of this response in Plato's dialogues, our principal source for it is Aristotle's account in *Metaphysics* books A, M and N. Since Aristotle recounts these doctrines in order to criticize them, some scholars argue that his reports are not reliable; all readers find them difficult to understand. Nonetheless, because he does propose, on behalf of the Academy, a response to Parmenides that he regards as important, readers of the *Metaphysics* should appreciate it. According to Aristotle, Plato and the Academy try to construct things from both the character common to all beings, namely, "the one itself," and its contrary. The contrary of the one itself is not "the many" as this latter is usually understood, for that many is a plurality of ones and, thus, presupposes the one itself instead of opposing it. Instead, they take the contrary to be an indeterminate many that lacks unity in any sense. They call it the "indefinite dyad." This phrase is famously obscure, but the idea behind it is not. Think of a group of things that belong to the same class. They have something in common, the character that defines the class, but they must each also have some characteristic that distinguishes them from each other and from this common, defining character. Since the common defining character is a source of shared determination, the distinguishing character of each thing must be indeterminate. Thus, each individual is composed of the defining character and some indeterminate difference. Since the difference cannot be a single entity without partaking of the one, the Academy thinks of it as a dyad. Thus, it is possible to say that all things are composed of a determination and an indeterminacy or, as it is more typically put, of the one and the indefinite dyad. For Plato's school, these latter are the principles of all things. Different people in the school worked out the details differently, proposing various hierarchical arrangements in accordance with different degrees of determinacy; but all seem to have thought that all things are, in some important sense, in the same class.

As such, all things come under a single science, that is, a single branch of knowledge. On the other hand, the Platonists also recognize the existence of particular sciences or arts. In his dialogue *Philebus*, Plato distinguishes the philosopher's arithmetic from the arithmetic of the many (56d). In the former, all the units are equal; in the latter the units are cattle or armies or other things that are unequal. Whereas the philosopher counts equal units, the herdsman counts cattle, the general armies. Nonetheless, all the arts and sciences use counting and measuring, though some do so more than others. Thus, building and music depend heavily on mathematics, whereas military strategy and agriculture make less use of mathematics. Plato suggests a hierarchy of sciences based on the degree to which they use mathematics. At the top of the hierarchy is the philosopher's arithmetic. It is followed closely by pure calculation (the science of making calculations with pure units) and geometry. Next are the arts like building and music that use mathematics extensively but impurely, and last the arts that make relatively little use of mathematics. It follows that someone who knows the philosopher's arithmetic knows the basis of all the arts. If the one and the indefinite dyad are the principles of pure numbers, then the person who knows these principles knows all the arts and sciences. Conversely, knowing any particular science requires knowing something about number and measurement and, thereby, something about the first principles of all things. This account of the relationship between the one science (metaphysics) that knows all things by knowing the first principles and the particular sciences that know the principles of more limited subject matters is implicit in the *Philebus*.

In other dialogues Plato has Socrates raise questions about the relationship between a first science and subordinate sciences as objections to the existence of metaphysics. There are two sorts of objections: (1) If each subject matter is known by some particular science, there is no subject left for the highest science to know; but there is no science without its own proper subject matter. (2) If each science has a product (housebuilding produces the house, shoemaking the shoes, etc.), and the science that uses the product is higher than the science that makes it, then the highest science could not have a product. (If it did, then any science that used its product would be still higher, and we would have to inquire into the science that uses its product, and so on.) However, a highest science with no product would serve no end and, thus, be worthless.

Plato resolves these problems by identifying a distinctive *subject matter* for the highest sciences, separate forms. Since, as he argues, everything else imitates these forms, one who knows them knows something about everything else. He is able to *produce* things that imitate the forms, things like city-states, virtuous souls, and even physical objects. Again, there is a single generic science that knows all things by knowing their principles (that is, the forms) and specific sciences that each know a species of the genus of all things.

Aristotle argues against this account of the one and the many sciences, and he offers his own account in the *Metaphysics*. However, it is important to realize that he recognizes the force of the problem. If there is to be one architectonic science of all things, it must somehow have its own subject matter, and it must somehow govern the other sciences. The problem of metaphysics is whether there is such a science. Hence, the problem of metaphysics is intrinsically a problem of how there can be one science that stands over all other sciences. Metaphysics is the only science that wrestles with its own existence, and its existence turns on finding some one thing or type of thing that stands over all other things and, thus, some one science that stands over all other sciences. Metaphysics is intrinsically connected with the problem of the one and the many that Aristotle's predecessors address.

Aristotelian science

The term "science" is now often used loosely for an organized body of knowledge for which there is strong evidence, specifically the knowledge of nature and mathematical entities. Even though Aristotle uses this term for a broader range of subjects, he has more specific criteria for its application. A science (or, equivalently, "branch of knowledge") (1) knows unchanging objects (2) that are grasped through their cause. The key to understanding how Aristotle meets these criteria lies in understanding the standard form of argument, the syllogism. The canonical syllogism, nicknamed "Barbara," has the following form:

All M is P.
All S is M.
Therefore, All S is P.

M here is the middle term. We can say that we know that all S is P through M. Hence, M plays the role of a cause. The canonical *scientific* syllogism is a particular interpretation of the canonical syllogism. Here, S is the subject genus and P is an essential attribute. M is the essential nature of the genus. Hence, the syllogism shows that an essential attribute belongs to a genus because of the latter's essential nature. A genus is a class of things that all have the same essential nature. For an attribute to belong to a genus is for it to be in each instance of the genus. For example: every rational animal is a being that is able to store food internally long enough to learn; every human being is a rational animal; hence, every human being is a being that is able to store food internally long enough to learn. Since the internal organ in which we store food is the long intestine, this syllogism is part of an Aristotelian account of why we have a long intestine.

It is often said that Aristotle does not follow his own scientific method in his physical and biological works. However, this remark misunderstands how Aristotle uses the syllogism. It assumes that he envisions science as a deductive enterprise, as if the essential attributes could somehow be deduced from a generic nature. Instead, Aristotle claims that scientific inquiry seeks the middle term, the M. That is to say, Aristotle uses the syllogism not to go from premises to conclusion, but to search in the opposite direction. His science begins from the observation that various attributes belong to a genus; that is, science begins from the *conclusion* of the syllogism. It aims to find the cause in respect of which the attributes belong to the genus; this cause is the genus's essential nature. In general, scientific inquiry seeks to find the essential nature that defines its subject genus, the M. The syllogism directs the inquiry by showing what needs to be found. Sometimes Aristotle says that scientific inquiry begins from what is "prior for us" and finds what is "prior in nature." The syllogism's conclusion is prior for us because it is a matter of observation; the syllogism's middle term is prior in nature. It is grasped through intellect. Thus, to return to the example of the previous paragraph, Aristotle begins with the observation that all human beings have long intestines, and seeks a cause, an M, that accounts for this fact. This cause is our rational nature, for to use reason we need extended periods of time when we are not eating and, thus, need an internal organ that can store food.

Aristotle's account of science is more rigid than modern accounts because he is concerned to answer Plato's contention that sensibles cannot be known. Both philosophers think that (a) the object of knowledge cannot change and also that (b) sensibles are always changing. These two assumptions lead Plato to conclude that sensibles cannot be objects of knowledge. Aristotle avoids this conclusion by arguing that these sensibles have unchanging essential natures as well as attributes that necessarily belong to them in respect of these natures. Thus, although individual sensibles change, their genera do not. (We will see later that he argues that sensibles have essential natures.) In other words, the syllogistic structure that Aristotle ascribes to science allows changing sensibles to be known by their unchanging natures, attributes, and genera.

Since metaphysics seeks the highest causes, we might think that it would seek that essential nature, M, that is the cause of the essential properties of *all* things. However, there is no genus of all things, as we will see later. Even if there were such a genus, its essential nature would not be the highest cause, but the lowest cause. To see why, consider the genus of animals. The generic nature of animals is the capacity for sensation. This character belongs to each instance of the genus, and it accounts for every animal's having sense organs and, perhaps, for its being able to move itself. But each species of animal has its own sorts of sense organs and characteristic ways of movement. Whereas the generic nature of the genus animal accounts for characteristics common to all animals, the specific nature of, say, mammals, accounts for sense organs peculiar to mammals as well as hair, eyebrows, and other characteristics of this species. Each mammal has these latter essential attributes in virtue of its being a mammal. It has other, more general attributes insofar as it is an animal. Since each mammal is also an animal, the cause of its being a mammal is also the cause of its being an animal. So the essential nature of mammals is the cause not only of the essential attributes specific to mammals but also of the general attributes that belong to all animals. Insofar as the essential nature of mammals causes those attributes that are also caused by the essential nature of animal, it is the higher cause. This is an important point: the higher cause is the cause of the more narrow universal. The cause of a species is higher than the cause of its genus. Suppose, now, that there were somehow a genus of all beings with its own generic nature. Since this genus is the broadest possible class, its generic nature would be *lowest* cause. On the other hand, a highest cause would be the essential nature of a narrow species. This latter cause could account for attributes essential to this species and also for the more general attributes that belong to it, but it could not account for the general attributes of beings.

It follows that a science of metaphysics could not be the standard sort of science Aristotle usually conceives. First, to be a science of *all* beings is at odds with being a science of the *highest* causes. Second, since Aristotle thinks that (a) each science has a genus as its subject matter and that (b) being is not a genus, it should follow that there is no science of being. The subject matter that metaphysics treats, all beings, cannot, apparently, be the object of a single science. It should follow that metaphysics does not exist as an Aristotelian science. If metaphysics does somehow exist as a science, it cannot have the same structure as a standard Aristotelian science.

The questions "whether metaphysics exists" and, if so, "how" are at issue in the *Metaphysics*. As noted earlier, metaphysics is the only science that wrestles with its own existence. Other sciences just assume the existence of a subject genus and its essential attributes. Aristotle needs to show that metaphysics can somehow treat all beings even if they do not constitute a genus. Further, he needs to show that there are some things that somehow serve as the causes or principles of all beings even if they are not the essential natures of those beings. Again, these causes are not abstractions or formulae, but things, and all other things, including sensibles, are somehow known through these highest causes. These two issues, subject matter and principles, are at the core of metaphysical inquiry.

Questions for reflection:

1 How does Aristotle's "cause" differ from a formula, a law, and an explanation?

2 How does Aristotle's idea of a science contrast with contemporary notions of science?

CHAPTER TWO

Overview of themes

The science of metaphysics has three tasks to accomplish. The *Metaphysics* divides neatly into three distinct parts, each of which accomplishes one of the tasks by introducing an original metaphysical doctrine. However, Aristotle does not announce these tasks or signal that he is undertaking them or that they have been completed. He gives readers very little guidance on how the text is organized. The order and symmetry of the whole can only be grasped by careful study and reflection. Individual passages in his text often appear disconnected from what surrounds them and difficult to understand on their own. Having an overview of the text gives the reader a context that helps to make these passages intelligible. Even so, the reader should not expect to understand the details of the text without a considerable effort. On the other hand, grasping the overview is challenging in a different way: because the tasks are defined by Aristotle's understanding of science, they are hard to grasp and appreciate. This chapter aims to show the enduring issues that motivate these tasks and to sketch Aristotle's solutions. In the process, more of his terminology must be explained. Although this chapter is best read before the next, the reader is advised that it will be more intelligible after working carefully through the next chapter.

The three tasks of metaphysics

The first task of metaphysics is to show that metaphysics exists as a science. As we saw in the previous chapter, to be an Aristotelian science, metaphysics needs to have its own subject matter, it needs principles (causes) through which this subject matter can be grasped, and it needs to be able to demonstrate attributes that belong to this subject matter in respect of the principles. Since metaphysics is supposed to be the highest science and, accordingly, to know the highest causes, that is, the causes of all beings, metaphysics should have all beings in its subject matter. The problem is that all beings do not constitute a genus, that is, a single class with a common nature, and Aristotle assumes that the subject matter of a science must be a genus. Moreover, there are additional objections to including particular entities together in a single science: there are reasons to deny that all the causes belong to one science, that all the substances belong to one science, and, likewise, all the attributes and the principles of demonstration. If all these could *not* be treated by one science, there would not be a science of metaphysics. That is to say, whether or not metaphysics exists hinges on the question of whether the things such a science treats could constitute the subject matter of a single science. Like Kant, Aristotle is, in effect, inquiring into how a metaphysics is possible, but for him the issue is not how there can be *a priori* knowledge of the world, but whether all things can be the subject matter of a science. In order to be known by one science, all beings must somehow share a single nature. So the task is to show *that* there is some nature that is common to all things.

The second task of metaphysics is to inquire into the nature of this subject matter, "what is being?" Since there is no one nature that belongs to every being, to ask this question is to seek that nature *through which* things are said to be; that is, it is to seek the primary being. This primary being is in the class of beings called "substance," that is, the class of self-subsistent beings. The term "substance" is called a "category" insofar as it is predicated of a class of beings. The class is a genus; indeed, it is one of the most inclusive genera. Other such genera, "categorial genera," include quality, quantity, and relation. Since instances of these latter exist as attributes of substances, they are known through substances. Since, though, these substances, sensible substances, are composites, it is necessary to ask, what is primary within them? That is, what is within them that makes each of them be the substance that it is. Hence, to ask "what is being?" is, ultimately, to seek that thing within substances that makes them be what they are, for this is primary among substances and, thereby, primary among all beings. In other words, to ask "what is being?" is to ask, "what is it for a substance to be?" and, indirectly, "what is it for any being to be?" In the course of finding what is primary among substances, Aristotle must also address the question of *which* things are substances.

The third task of metaphysics is to determine which substance is primary. The second task found what is "primary *among* substances," but this is an internal constituent of sensible substances that, we will see, does not exist without other constituents. In contrast, a "primary substance" is an entity that does not require something else in order to exist. It is obvious that the latter must be eternal because if it came into being, its existence would depend on some other cause. There are many candidates for primary substance, each with some claim to legitimacy by virtue of being eternal. Aristotle needs to decide which has the best claim, but he also needs to show how the other candidates depend on the primary substance or substances. Mathematical entities like lines and planes are plausible candidates for primary substances because they have seemed to exist independently while also forming the defining boundaries of physical substances, and the one that is the principle of number is an even stronger candidate. Both receive a great deal of attention even though they are shown not to be primary substances. In short, the third task is to find that substance that is the highest cause of all substances and, thereby, of all beings.

How metaphysics accomplishes its three tasks

With this brief sketch of what a science of metaphysics needs to do, we can outline how the *Metaphysics* actually completes these tasks. The book opens by discussing, first, our apparently human impulse to seek to know the causes of things, an impulse that pushes us toward the highest causes (A.1) and, second, the character of the wisdom possessed by someone who grasps these highest causes (A.2). The rest of book A describes four general types of causes (A.3), argues that there are no more than these cause types by showing that all the causes that other philosophers have proposed are instances of these four (A.3–7), and shows the inadequacy of some proposed causes, notably those of Plato and the Academy (A.8–9). The second book of the *Metaphysics*, α, argues that there are no infinite sequences of causes. Since there are four types of causes, and since within each type there cannot be an infinite sequence, there are first causes. Both A and α investigate *all* the causes. Among these causes are the highest causes of all things. Hence, the study of all the causes is also the study of the causes of all things. Aristotle terms this latter "wisdom"; his editor calls it "metaphysics." The first two books serve to show that there is a science of metaphysics by themselves exemplifying metaphysical investigation. This is important because it means that all the objections raised to the existence of metaphysics can be answered. To be sure, these objections must be stated and explored, and Aristotle needs to show how to undermine them, but it is clear that a science of metaphysics does exist.

Book B consists of a series of antinomies. They are called *"aporiai,"* a term that means lack of passage, because they stymie thought. They divide neatly into three sets. The first set concerns the existence of the science. The second set concerns the character of the principles of the science, whether they are separate and in what way they are one. The third set wrestles with issues that surround the first principles, whether particular entities that have some claim to be the primary beings are indeed primary. That is to say, the *aporiai* fall into three groups that raise obstacles to the three tasks that metaphysics must complete. In the rest of the *Metaphysics* Aristotle resolves these *aporiai* by removing the obstacles.

He resolves the first set of *aporiai* in books Γ–Δ and, in doing so, shows that metaphysics exists. The existence of metaphysics is declared in the first sentence of book Γ: "There is a science that studies being *qua* being and what belongs to it *per se.*" This is a conclusion. Aristotle argues for it by showing in successive arguments how one science can treat the topics that must fall under metaphysics. That is to say, the reason for denying the existence of metaphysics is that distinct sorts of beings must, apparently, be treated in distinct sciences. By showing how they can fall under a *single* science, Aristotle is removing the reason for denying the existence of metaphysics. He shows that metaphysics exists by showing that its subject matter has enough unity to be treated by one science. The arguments are clearly marked in the text, but readers usually overlook them because their conclusions assert that there is *one* science of some subject matter. Aristotle shows that the science is one in order to show that it *is*, and the science is one because, despite arguments to the contrary, its subject matter is one.

In order that the subject matter be known to be one, it must be knowable; and to be knowable, it must be subject to the principle of non-contradiction (PNC), the highest principle of knowledge. In its simplest form the principle asserts that the same thing cannot be and not be at the same time, in the same way. Although Aristotle appears, on a straightforward reading of Γ.3–8, to be arguing for the PNC, he also shows that any argument for the principle must presuppose it. Hence, this section should be understood not as an argument for the principle, but as an analysis of what must be the case if the principle is to hold: what nature must all things have if it is true of each that it cannot be and not be at the same time, in the same way? Speaking as if he were arguing for the PNC, Aristotle claims that in order to show that the principle holds, it is necessary to assume that a term signifies one nature. Thus, "man" must signify two-footed animal or something of this sort. If "man" also signifies the contradictory, that is, whatever is *not* a two-footed animal, then it signifies one of these no more than the other. It follows that whatever is said of man could equally be said of not-man, and a claim that is true of the one is equally true of the other. Obviously, there can be no knowledge of man. If, on the contrary, "man" does signify just one nature, then it is not the case that it also signifies its contradictory. In this case, there is no obstacle to knowing the nature of man. The implicit conclusion is that in order to be subject to the principle of non-contradiction and, thereby, to be capable of being known, things must have natures.

Strikingly, Aristotle argues that the principle extends to *every* being. Hence, every being has a nature and can be known. (This conclusion contrasts sharply with Plato's view that sensibles have no natures of their own and, therefore, cannot be known.) Insofar as it has its own nature, each being is a sort of substance. What makes something a being is, evidently, to have a nature. Having a nature is, in effect, a character common to all beings. This character is not a determinate nature like man or three. It is not a nature that falls into one of the genera of being. Nonetheless, insofar as every being does have its own nature, all are alike and can be treated together. Moreover, certain attributes belong to each being simply because it has a nature; namely, attributes like unity, sameness, relation, priority or posteriority, and the other attributes that Aristotle explores in book Δ. All of being can be treated by one science, namely, metaphysics, because being has a character that functions as an essence would and attributes that belong in respect of this essence. Aristotle describes being as "*pros hen,*" which means literally "related to one." This Greek phrase is sometimes rendered as "focal meaning," and scholars usually supposed that the "one" from which all beings derive their meaning is the categorial genus of substance. Later in the *Metaphysics*, Aristotle does use "*pros hen*" like this, but here in book Γ his point is rather that all beings do have something in common insofar as *each* has a nature.

In short, Aristotle shows that metaphysics exists by showing that its subject matter, all beings, constitutes a kind of genus and, thereby, falls under one science. He shows, in effect, *that* being is because there is a nature of being that can be known. Metaphysics' second task is to determine what this nature is, that is, to determine *what* being is. In other words, what makes a being be what it is? The *Posterior Analytics* (book II, ch. 2) distinguishes two scientific questions, the "is it?" and the "what is it?" questions. In general, these questions are answered together by finding a nature that is shared by all instances of the genus. The existence of some common nature proves *that* the genus is, and this nature is also *what* the genus is. Most sciences begin by assuming a subject genus and, then, show *that* it is and *what* it is by finding a single nature that is shared by each instance of this genus. Thus, zoology assumes the genus of animal and then finds the single nature that makes each thing in the genus be an animal.

In metaphysics, however, the "is it?" question is answered independently of the "what is it?" question. Metaphysics Γ–Δ show *that* the class of all beings functions as a subject genus for metaphysics. Books E–Θ determine *what* being is. Whereas the answer to the former question focuses on what is common to all beings, namely, having a nature, the answer to the latter explores different things that are the nature of being. "'Being' is said in many ways," Aristotle claims in Δ.7. He means that different sorts of things are said to be: (1) conjunctions of different sorts of beings count as beings, but they are usually beings accidentally; (2) truths, (3) the categories, and (4) actuality/potentiality are beings essentially. Aristotle explores these four "ways of being" in, respectively: (1) E.2–3, (2) E.4 and Θ.10, (3) Z–H, (4) Θ.1–9.

There is no knowledge of accidental beings. So, that way of being is set aside. In each other way of being, Aristotle looks to find the being that is primary. The primary being is that thing in respect of which other things are said to be in the same way. Thus, among categorial beings Aristotle seeks a primary being, that categorial being through whose nature other categorial beings are said to be. Likewise, among truths Aristotle seeks a primary being, and among actualities and potentialities he seeks a primary being.

Truths in thoughts and words depend upon truths in things, and Aristotle, accordingly, sets them aside until the latter are discussed (E.4). The treatment of categorial beings is complicated, but it is clear first that the natures of all the other categories depend upon and, thus, include the nature of substance. A substance, in turn, is said to be in respect of several different features. Aristotle's strategy is to set out what are widely recognized as substances (Z.2) and also the characters in respect of which they are said to be substances (Z.3). Examining the latter one by one, he eliminates some of them and identifies the remainder with each other. By considering which character is itself one and makes the thing one, he is able to determine that character that is the cause of anything's being a substance. This character is the nature of substance and, thus, of being. It is the thing's essence or, equivalently, its form; and form, Aristotle argues, is actuality. (As the next section will explain, an "actuality" is something like a thing's function.) That is to say, what makes something be a substance is its form, and that form is its actuality.

This conclusion is consonant with the treatments of the other two ways of being. Something is a potentiality in respect of an actuality, and there is an actuality in respect of which other things are actualities, namely, the actuality of a substance. The latter is the form of the substance. Likewise, things are true if they are united in the way that a substance and its essential attribute are united. What is true most of all are things that are simple; they are grasped all at once and do not admit of falsity. These simples are, of course, actualities.

It follows that the nature that is primary among each of the essential ways of being is the form or actuality of a substance. Because every being is what it is in respect of this form, form is the nature of being. At least, this is the nature of *sensible* being, for the ways of being that Aristotle discusses in books E–Θ are all ways in which sensibles are said to be.

This latter observation helps to explain the third task of metaphysics, to find the first principle; for nothing that is sensible can be the first principle. Each sensible contains matter. As we will see, anything with matter requires something else either to cause its form to be present in its matter or to move the matter. Either way, the sensible being is not a first principle or cause. Aristotle canvasses a number of candidates for the first principle before settling, famously, on the unmoved movers. One reason that they are plausible first principles is that they are causes of motion, whereas other supposed first principles are not. These other principles are, nonetheless, principles. In particular, they are principles of science (that is, principles of knowledge) and principles of number. In order for the unmoved movers to be truly first, they must somehow serve as the principle of the other candidates for first principle. Hence, Aristotle spends much of the last third of the *Metaphysics* discussing the principles of number and of figures along with the one. He needs to show that the unmoved movers are principles not only of sensible substances but also of numbers, Platonic forms, and other candidates for first principles.

Book I shows both that there is no one itself of the sort Parmenides posits as a principle and also that the one exists as a kind of analogy and is, thereby, dependent on the natures of different kinds of beings. Book K serves to reinterpret the search for a first cause. Whereas the central books had located a cause within sensible substances that is not a self-subsistent being, this book along with Λ.1–5 shows that the first principle should be a self-subsistent cause of motion. Λ.6–10 argues for and expounds the nature of such a cause or, as it emerges, causes. They are Aristotle's own first principles, the unmoved movers. M.1–3 argues that geometric objects cannot be first principles and also shows how they exist. M.4–5 argues against Platonic forms being first principles, and M.10 shows that these forms are, rather, universals that exist potentially in sensibles. M.6–9 argues against form numbers – a version of the Platonic form account proposed by the Academy and possibly Plato – being first principles. Book N argues against the one and the indefinite dyad – also principles proposed by the Academy – being the principles from which number and all else are derived, and it also shows how numbers exist in sensibles.

We might expect Aristotle's own first principles to be causes from which sensible substances are produced or derived. Were this so, it might be possible to deduce the nature of a sensible substance from the nature of its principle. Aristotle does not think such a deduction is possible. His unmoved movers are, instead, causes of stable patterns of motion. They move the heavenly spheres so that these latter move – eternally, Aristotle thinks – in their orbits. These spheres are responsible for the seasons and the regular patterns of plant and animal development. The unmoved movers are final causes. They are the ends that the heavenly spheres strive to imitate through motion. Always moving in circles, the spheres are, in a way, always the same and, thereby, imitate an entity that is entirely without motion. These heavenly spheres are themselves imitated by the cycle of plant and animal life on earth. Yet, we cannot determine the nature of any sensible being from its first cause. There is an unbridgeable gap between the nature of this principle and the nature of that of which it is a principle. The principle accounts for things striving to continue to be what they are, but not for the nature that they are.

There is, accordingly, a fundamental diversity in the world that Aristotle does not think can be unified. In consequence, metaphysical knowledge of the principles of all things is not a knowledge of the principles important for the particular sciences. This fact means that there is a role for metaphysics that is independent of the particular sciences and that does not contribute directly to individual sciences.

Three central doctrines

The three tasks of metaphysics are accomplished by means of three central doctrines, one for each task. This section sketches the doctrines and mentions how they contribute toward accomplishing the tasks.

The first doctrine is the notion that being is a *pros hen*. Sometimes termed "focal meaning," this doctrine asserts that a particular type of thing and all that is related to it constitute a kind of class and are, consequently, called by the same term. Aristotle illustrates it with "healthy." There is a central core, "health," to which different things are related in different ways. Diet can contribute to health, complexion can be a sign of health, and the body is receptive to health. These relations to health have nothing in common with each other except that they are relations to health, yet all can be grasped somehow through health. The class of things related to health is termed "healthy." Again, this class is not understood through a single character that each instance of the class possesses, as each instance of the genus of animal possesses the essential nature of animal. Instead, it is understood as what is related to a single nature.

The significance of this doctrine is that a *pros hen* class can be treated by an Aristotelian science. Aristotle regularly claims that one science treats one genus. We have seen why in the previous chapter. However, Aristotle notes that the science of medicine does not confine itself to health. It treats everything related to health, that is, the healthy. He reasons that if this *pros hen* can be the subject matter of a science, then any *pros hen* could be the subject matter of a science. In the strict sense a "genus" is a class, like animal, in which each instance shares an essential nature, but Aristotle also recognizes a broad sense of this term in which it refers to a *pros hen* class. This expanded usage allows him to continue to affirm that one science treats one genus, for "genus" now has both a strict and a broad sense.

As noted, there is no nature common to all beings. However, if being is a *pros hen*, it could be the subject of a science. Since there is a science of metaphysics, as we know from books A and α, and since metaphysics must somehow know all beings if it is to know the highest causes of all beings, there must be a science that somehow encompasses all beings. Since this is possible if being is a *pros hen* and, it seems, in no other way, being must be a *pros hen*. In effect, the *pros hen* doctrine expands the meaning of "genus" to allow the broader subject matter necessary for there to be a science of metaphysics. Aristotle's point in book Γ of the *Metaphysics* is that even if there is no one determinate nature that each being possesses, all beings do constitute enough of a unified class to be treated by one science. Later, in the central books, that is, in *Metaphysics* E–Θ, when he inquires into the nature of being, he shifts his attention from the unity of the class of all beings to the nature to which other beings are related.

The second key doctrine is that form is actuality. What makes a thing be a thing? Whatever else must be said about it, a thing is one. Its material parts constitute a single entity. What is the cause of this entity's being one? Whatever it is that unifies its diverse parts. This unifier cannot be another material constituent, for then the same problem would arise: what is it that unifies *all* the material constituents, this one along with all the others? To avoid regress, it is necessary that the unifier be something that is not material, such as a form. The parts of a house stacked on the ground and the standing house do not differ in their material. They differ in that in the house, the material is organized and able to function as a house. The form of the house is present in the matter. Of course, even when they are stacked on the ground, the house parts have some form, though not the form of the house. The difference is that when the parts are organized into a house, they can perform the function of the house, providing shelter. Evidently, what makes a thing be what it is is its capacity for a characteristic function. The house is an artifact, not a substance: its function is for the sake of the user. In a substance, the function *is* its own end. Thus, the parts of a plant are unified insofar as they function together, and their functioning together is just the end of the plant. This type of functioning is what Aristotle calls an "actuality."

The third key doctrine is the nature of actuality. Since a function is an actuality, it is easiest for contemporary readers to think of an actuality as a kind of motion. But Aristotle sharply distinguishes these two. A motion has an end in something else. When this end is reached, the motion ceases. Thus, the end of the motion of house-building lies in the finished house, and the motion ceases when the house is finished. All motions would come to an end unless they are sustained by something else, as in the case of eternal circular motions of the heavens. In contrast, an actuality is its own end. Hence, it never winds down or ceases, though it may no longer be present in a matter. The actuality that is a plant's nature does exist in a matter. It must come to be in matter and cease to be there at some point, but it does not itself change in doing so. An actuality that comes to exist with matter requires a cause. Hence, it cannot be the first cause.

An actuality that exists without matter does not require another cause. Hence, it need not have a prior cause. Further, such a pure actuality is an end – things move in order to attain a stability that imitates it. Hence, an actuality that does not exist in matter can be a first cause. It remains to show that such an actuality can account for the other candidates claiming to be first causes. Aristotle must also prove that a pure actuality exists as an entity. Clearly, issues need to be addressed, but it is possible, at least, to conceive of a first cause.

The first cause accounts for the motions of sensible natures. It does not account for the characters those natures have. A thing's nature belongs to the thing and causes its parts to be one. The motions that must take place in order that a nature be present in its matter depend ultimately on a first cause, but what the nature is does not. Hence, the account of the first cause does not remove the need for accounts of the lower causes. Even so, there are two distinct accounts of these lower causes. A metaphysical account of the lower causes focuses on the unity of form and matter because it is this that makes the composite be. However, form and matter are one only "in a way." In another way, they remain distinct. Aristotle needs this difference to account for motion, for motion occurs when a form comes to be in matter that is distinct from it. Thus, a physical account of lower causes is possible because form and matter are not one, whereas the metaphysical account depends on their being one. Thus, metaphysics has a role to play as a branch of knowledge, but it does not undermine the other sciences. Besides justifying its own existence, metaphysics must show that other sciences are possible. Metaphysics contributes to these other sciences without undermining their integrity as distinct sciences.

CHAPTER THREE

Reading the text

A.1

The first sentence of the *Metaphysics* is: "all men by nature desire to know." Like the first sentences of many other chapters of this work, this one is a conclusion. In the rest of chapter 1 of book A, Aristotle gives three arguments for it: (1) We value our senses, especially sight. The senses belong to us by nature, and they are sources of knowledge. Hence, we naturally value knowledge. (2) Often the person who has learned to do something by experience performs as well or better than the person who has learned by mastering the theory. Yet, we still respect the latter more than the former because of his knowledge. (Aristotle's example is the doctor in contrast with the person who has experience treating diseases but does not understand their causes.) Hence, we value knowledge. (3) The priests of Egypt developed mathematics after the other arts, those that met necessities and provided pleasures, had been developed. Since their physical needs were met, they were free to pursue knowledge. Those whose time is their own would, like the Egyptian priests, pursue knowledge. Hence, man by nature desires to know.

The first argument concerns the lowest type of knowledge, knowledge from the senses. According to this argument, even watching football games and following fire trucks are manifestations of the desire to know. The second argument contrasts lower types of knowledge, that is, knowledge from sense and experience, with the higher types, art and science. Interestingly, it is the *lack* of practical benefit from higher knowledge that Aristotle takes to signify our interest in knowledge for its own sake. The third argument also emphasizes theoretical knowledge that Aristotle thinks of no practical value.

Most readers will be inclined to reject Aristotle's notion that our interest in knowledge is not practical. The sciences and mathematics have greatly improved human life. Indeed, according to other accounts, the ancient Egyptians developed geometry to settle land disputes that arose after the annual flooding of the Nile. However, Aristotle is not denying that knowledge *can* be useful. His point is that there is some knowledge that is not of any use but, nonetheless, highly valued. A case in point is the respect accorded to those who have mastered such arcane branches of knowledge as Chinese history, literary theory, and theoretical astrophysics. That we value useful knowledge is understandable, but why should we value knowledge that has no utility? There is no explanation other than that we value knowledge for its own sake. Because our respect for knowledge has no other cause, Aristotle roots it in human nature.

When we seek to know for some other purpose, there is no reason to seek further knowledge once the purpose is attained. If, though, our desire to know stems from human nature, our pursuit of knowledge is not limited. Whenever we discover a reason, we can continue to ask for a reason for that reason. Thus, because our desire to know is natural, we seek the highest sort of knowledge, the knowledge of first causes. This is metaphysics.

It was surely as obvious to Aristotle as it is to us that not all people are actively seeking knowledge of metaphysics. Readers will readily think of friends who seem to have little interest in any knowledge, and they might wonder to whom the "we" of Aristotle's arguments refers. Aristotle would not be concerned with apparent exceptions. For one, few people have the leisure to pursue knowledge or the ability to discover first causes. Then, too, Aristotle says that all desire to know, not to learn. Learning is often hard work. Most of us quickly grow tired of seeking causes and settle for the more easily acquired knowledge from the senses. Again, Aristotle would regard anyone asking who won a football game as supporting his thesis, assuming the inquirer has not bet on the game. Often, students say that they have come to college for its practical benefits, but it is extraordinary how many people study philosophy and how much respect is paid to eminent scholars whose knowledge has not the least practical benefit. If Aristotle's arguments are sound, our nature is to desire not knowledge for its practical benefit, but practical benefit in order to have the leisure to pursue knowledge, like the Egyptian priests. For most people, Aristotle is advancing a profound re-evaluation of human life.

Questions for reflection:

1 Is knowledge valuable for its own sake? If knowledge is always valuable for the sake of something else, for what is that valuable? And for what else is that valuable? Can we ever arrive at something that is not valuable for something else, but valuable in itself?

2 Aristotle implies that our natural desire for knowledge could be satisfied only with the ultimate knowledge, knowledge of first causes. Has he shown that there are such causes?

A.2

Aristotle thinks that "common opinions" (*endoxa*), the opinions that are held widely and, especially, those that are held by the wise, are generally right, though they often need to be refined. As a way to understand the nature of metaphysics, a science he here calls "wisdom," he recounts common opinions about those who have this science. In particular, this chapter discusses six characteristics said to belong to the wise man and his wisdom: (1) he knows all things, to the extent possible; (2) his knowledge is difficult to attain; (3) his knowledge is more accurate; (4) he is more able to teach causes; (5) his knowledge is desirable for itself rather than its results; (6) his knowledge is superior to other kinds of knowledge and orders them.

Criterion (1) is met if the object of knowledge is most universal, that is, if it is a class, like being, that includes all things. The more inclusive and, thus, more universal a class is, the further removed it is from sensation and therefore the more difficult it is to grasp, thereby meeting criterion (2). On the other hand, knowledge that is (3) most accurate and (4) teachable is the knowledge of the causes that are the most simple. These criteria might seem to be met by knowing an individual or a species, like "man," that is least inclusive, in contrast with species like animal that are more inclusive. Arithmetic, for example, is simpler than geometry and, thus, prior to geometry. However, a universal, like "being," a universal that includes all things, is simple insofar as it is not composed of other universals. There is nothing more universal from which it could be composed. In contrast, a lower universal, like "man," is *not* simple because it is composed of two other universals, namely, animal and rational. Criteria (5) and (6) seem to be at odds because a knowledge valued for its own sake would not be useful, whereas a science that enables its possessor to order other sciences would be useful. However, Aristotle argues that knowledge of first principles and causes is valuable for its own sake because they are most knowable in themselves, whereas knowledge of other principles is *not* valuable (merely) for its own sake because in knowing these lesser principles, we know the first principles upon which they depend. Furthermore, insofar as the first principles and causes are the end of all things, someone who knows them is able to properly appreciate the subordinate value of other kinds of knowledge. Hence, Aristotle concludes that a single science can meet all the criteria of wisdom, the science that knows the first principles and causes. He assumes that these latter are the highest universals.

It is at this point that Aristotle says, famously, that philosophy begins in wonder. We wonder when one line cannot be put into numeric proportion with another (namely, the hypotenuse of a right isosceles triangle with its side), or when marionettes appear to move themselves. Our wonder disappears, however, once we understand their causes, that is, the reason the diagonal is incommensurable and that strings move the marionettes. The suggestion here is that the wonder that occasions metaphysics will also be eliminated once the highest causes are discovered. Later, however, Aristotle claims that the question of being is always puzzling (Z.1.1028b2–4). Eventually he arrives at a first cause that, because its eternity is like nothing we experience, remains wondrous even when we grasp it (Λ.7.1072b24–26).

It is helpful to contrast Aristotle's science that rules other sciences because it knows the highest causes of all things with other views of what could be called "ruling" knowledge. Many people think that human experience is the ultimate judge of knowledge, which is to say that knowledge is valuable only if it is useful. However, something is useful only if it serves some end, and if that end is itself valuable only because it, in turn, serves another end, we risk an infinite regress. Thus, a science cannot be the "ruling" knowledge unless it is some sort of end in itself. In the nineteenth century many philosophers identified the knowledge that is prior to all others as the knowledge of man, that is, of human nature. Other philosophers, especially in the Middle Ages, declared revealed theology to be prior to all other types of knowledge.

Questions for reflection:

1   What does Aristotle mean when he says that one science rules and orders others? Compare what Aristotle says here with the ruling knowledge in *Nicomachean Ethics* I.1–2 and with Plato's *Republic* 428b–d, 442c, 540a–b and *Euthydemus* 291c–292e. Is the ruling knowledge of the *Ethics* metaphysics?

2   Are the common opinions about the wise compatible with the types of "ruling" knowledge proposed by other philosophers?

The causes

A.3–7

Now that we know that metaphysics seeks the first causes, the obvious question is, what is a cause? Aristotle spends much of the rest of book A answering this question. He proceeds by example. In modern philosophy "cause" usually refers to the source of motion, the one billiard ball that moves another, the person who moves the first ball, or the person who made the billiard ball. This is one of Aristotle's causes, the "moving cause" or, as medieval thinkers called it, the "efficient cause." Aristotle identifies three other causes: a thing's matter, its form or essence, and its purpose.

The best way for us to understand the latter causes is to think of the kinds of things to be explained. If someone asks "Why is the statue heavy?" we might answer by mentioning its matter: "Because it is made of bronze." There is an implicit syllogism here. The matter, bronze, functions as its middle term, and outer terms are statue and heavy. It is a version of the Barbara syllogism we discussed in ch. 1, pp. 6–7: the statue is bronze; bronze is heavy; therefore, the statue is heavy. (Since a syllogism expresses a relation of classes, we must take "the statue" here to designate a class with a single instance.) On the other hand, if one asks, "Why is the statue tall and thin?", the answer could be "Because the statue depicts Abraham Lincoln." This answer refers to its form, and here form serves as the middle term of an implicit syllogism. If the question is, "Why did the statue come to be?" it might be answered "Because the sculptor made it." Finally, one could ask, "Why is the statue in the square?" and the answer might be "To inspire passers-by to noble deeds." This would be the purpose or final cause.

Modern philosophers like Descartes and Spinoza argue against final causes on the ground that, coming to exist only *after* an event occurs, they cannot play any role in the motion that brings it about. For Aristotelian science, though, the final cause is often the most important cause because it explains why, for example, an animal has the organs it does. If, for example, an animal's essence is or implies flying, then it must have wings or another such organ, it must have an organ able to support it while resting, and it must have still other organs to nourish these organs. In general, an animal's organs exist for the sake of its essential nature. The latter is not only its final cause, but its formal cause and, because it received its form from its parent, its efficient cause as well (see *Physics* II.7).

Aristotle's notion of matter is different from contemporary notions. He regards an animal's organs as its "matter," and this term is applied to any constituent part. Marble is a matter because it has the potential to be sculpted, even if this potential is not actualized. The premises of a syllogism are material for the conclusion. In modern (that is, seventeenth century) philosophy, "matter" comes to refer to a particular kind of thing, such as, something with extension or the stuff in which attributes inhere. However, Aristotle does not use "matter" to refer to a particular thing. He uses the term relationally: something is matter in respect of some form it takes on or as a part of some whole. Thus, even such immaterial entities as a genus or a line segment can be material causes. On the other hand, Aristotle considers a form to be immaterial even though it exists in matter.

Aristotle argues that there are only four causes by showing that all the causes that other philosophers had proposed fall under one of these four heads. Some causes, such as Heraclitus's fire and Parmenides' one, do not fall neatly under a single cause, but Aristotle thinks that that is because these philosophers were not thinking clearly. We do not possess the works that Aristotle is discussing. In fact, his discussion of his philosophical predecessors in *Metaphysics* A and the ancient commentaries on this discussion are important sources through which we know about the so-called "Presocratic Philosophers." Scholars agree that they were profound thinkers and that Aristotle's remarks do not convey their thought fully. But Aristotle is narrowly focused here on the issue of whether any of them are proposing a kind of causality that differs from one of his four kinds.

It is important to understand that a kind of cause is not the same as a particular cause within the kind. Water and air are distinct particular causes, though both belong to a single kind, material cause. The question "Is there one cause or many?" can be understood in two different ways: is there one *kind* of cause or many? or is there one *particular* cause or many? Aristotle is concerned with both interpretations. He distinguishes philosophers who advance a single material cause, such as Thales, from those who advance multiple material causes – Empedocles advances four. Likewise, some philosophers propose one pair of efficient causes, whereas others propose many pairs; and there seem to be proponents of a single formal cause and proponents of many formal causes.

Aristotle is also concerned to determine the number of *kinds* of causes. He notes that not only have different thinkers recognized different kinds of cause, but that there is a historical sequence of thought about these kinds. The earliest thinkers broke things down into their material constituents and claimed that they are causes. Eventually, other thinkers realized that there would also need to be moving causes to combine and separate these constituents. Hence, they introduced efficient causes in pairs, one to unify or move in one direction, the other to diversify or move in the opposite direction. When the constituents are unified they acquire a shape or structure – this is the form or formal cause. The end they serve in becoming unified is the final cause, the purpose. As noted, this end is often a thing's form.

This last point is very important for understanding an important difference between Aristotle's thought about causes and the modern view. When a modern author speaks about a cause, he has in mind some *distinct* thing that is responsible for producing an effect. That is to say, the cause of X is always something else, some Y whose existence precedes it in time. In contrast, Aristotle understands a cause to be something *within* a thing that sustains it as it is. Thus, the formal and material causes of a thing lie within it, as does its final cause if it is a nature, and they exist simultaneously with the thing. Its efficient cause does lie outside of it, but Aristotle insists that this cause is the same form that exists in the thing as its formal cause: your father has the same form as you do, and the artisan has in his mind the form that eventually comes to be in the artifact. In this way, Aristotle minimizes the externality of the efficient cause. To be sure, internal causes cannot account for every aspect of a thing. Ultimately, Aristotle argues for the existence of external causes that are first causes, but the need for such causes is not obvious because Aristotle supposes that each substance is somehow able to account for itself.

Since metaphysics is the science of the highest causes, the obvious question is, which kind of cause is the first cause? This question is not raised in book A. Instead, Aristotle focuses here on determining how many kinds of cause there are. As the number of causes becomes clear, so does the nature of each type. The account of their historical development helps to explain why four are sufficient.

Questions for reflection:

1 How does Aristotle's account of his causes implicitly explain why some things are self-subsistent?

2 Are final causes legitimate causes?

A.8–10

The last chapters of book A argue against the causes advanced by other philosophers. In A.8 Aristotle complains that those who advance material causes consider only the elements of bodies, not the elements of incorporeal entities. Further, they try to provide the causes of generation and destruction, but they omit the sources of motion and the substance that results from the motion. Even philosophers who do discuss the sources of motion and the conjunctions of elements limit the scope of their discussions to the causes of the generation and destruction of sensible substances and neglect imperceptible, incorporeal substances (989b21–27). Since the Pythagoreans advance numbers as causes, we might expect them to treat incorporeals; but, instead, they conceive of numbers as if they were sensible entities. Moreover, they use numbers to generate the heavens and to cause their motions. How can numbers, of any sort, cause motions? (So, even if the Pythagoreans did understand numbers as incorporeal, they could still not account for motion.) In any case, the Pythagoreans do not differ from the physical philosophers insofar as they offer physical causes to explain perceptible substances. Both groups of philosophers think that whatever exists is perceptible and is "contained by the so-called heavens."

In contrast, Plato's forms are truly incorporeal causes. Plato claims that they exist separately from all sensible beings. A.9 consists of a lengthy critique of Plato's account of the forms and of the accounts of others in Plato's school, the Academy. Among the famous arguments is Aristotle's claim that to assert that there are forms is like someone who, wanting to count things, decided that they would be easier to count if they were doubled. Aristotle thinks that a Platonic form is exactly like the sensible except that it is eternal and not sensible. Plato adds "itself" to the man to signal that he is not referring to any particular man, but to the form. That makes the form a distinct thing, but it does not add anything at all to what we know about man. The man is, as it were, doubled in a vain attempt to explain it. Another famous argument is that the same grounds for thinking that there are forms of sensibles are also grounds for concluding that there are forms of artifacts and of negations, forms that Platonists reject. More famous still is an argument Aristotle refers to here simply as "the third man." It is usually supposed to be something like the argument Plato discusses in his *Parmenides* (132a–b). If so, it would begin from our ability to recognize many men. If there are many men, there must be some one nature in respect of which we judge each of them to be a man. This nature serves as a standard. It is the man that is common to all, that is, a "one over many," a form. As the form through which the many men are known, it is distinct from this plurality of men. However, the form man and the many men also constitute a plurality of men. In order to recognize them as such, there must be still another form, a third man, in respect of which each of them is a man. In short, the argument for the existence of a form of man can be reapplied to yield an indefinite number of forms. This is presumably the argument against the forms that Aristotle has in mind.

Another of his arguments is, I think, more incisive and not easily answered. Plato's separate forms are immaterial and unchanging. As such, they cannot cause motion in sensibles. That is to say, the nature that Plato ascribes to the forms renders them incapable of accounting for the sensibles and, thus, incapable of being causes. This last argument shows the contrast between Aristotle's other philosophical predecessors and Plato. Whereas the other philosophers focused on accounting for the motions of sensibles and ignored incorporeal beings, Plato gave an account of incorporeal beings that could not also account for the sensibles.

Scholars are divided on the effectiveness of Aristotle's arguments against the forms. Some argue that Aristotle trivializes Plato and fails to understand him. Others are convinced that the arguments are devastating. Whatever their effectiveness, Aristotle's arguments against Plato's forms serve to distinguish these forms from Aristotle's own forms. The two types of form are very close. For Plato the essential nature of a sensible being like a man lies in the form that exists apart from it, a form that is not sensible. Your nature is not you or anything that belongs to you, but something unchanging that exists separately – even though what is most characteristic of human life is growth and change. As we will see, Aristotle's own form lies within the thing and is a cause of the thing's motion. The problem with Plato's and the Academy's accounts of causes is that they are inadequate and incomplete. Again, the others' causes cannot account for incorporeals, and Plato's cannot account for sensibles. Because neither set of causes can account for all beings, neither can be the first causes. On the other hand, to ask whether something is the cause of everything and to seek such a cause is to engage in metaphysical inquiry. There is some reason to think that this science does exist.

Book α: an infinite number of causes?

There are no more than four kinds of causes, but how many individual causes are there? In particular, suppose that A is caused by B, B is caused by C, and C is caused by D; can such a sequence of causes continue indefinitely or must it always terminate in some first cause? The question is important because if there is no termination, then there is no first cause. Since metaphysics is the science of first causes, if all sequences of causes were without termination, there would be no metaphysics.

If the world exists for a finite time, causal sequences must terminate. They cannot extend past the beginning of the world. But Aristotle argues that the world is eternal, as we will see. It follows that causal sequences need not terminate. Moreover, since Aristotle thinks that a species is eternal, it would seem that some causal chains would have to be infinite: your parents caused you, their parents caused them, and so on indefinitely.

Aristotle, however, argues that no causal sequence is infinite. Every sequence has a beginning. He does not explain how there can be a beginning of causal sequences if each species and the world as a whole are eternal. We will see that an individual instance of a species is generated when a pre-existing form comes to be present in a pre-existing matter (Z.7). Although the individual's forebears stretch back infinitely, his existence does not depend on an infinite number of events because the causes at work in his generation, namely, form and matter, do not change in the generation. Similarly, although all sequences terminate, they do not terminate at the same time. There is an eternal cause that somehow initiates causal sequences at different times. The character of this first cause remains in the background in book α.

In this book Aristotle focuses on showing that causal sequences do not extend indefinitely. The first point to notice is that, because there are four different kinds of causes, there are four kinds of causal sequence. Aristotle considers each in turn. The general objection to an infinite sequence of causes (994a11–19) is that if there is no first cause, there cannot be anything to start the sequence. This problem is most pertinent to the case of efficient causes. Without a first, there is no sequence of efficient causes. Hence, there must be a first efficient cause.

There are two ways there could be a sequence of material causes:
(a) the matter could be potentially what it becomes, as a boy is the
matter of a man, or (b) the matter could be destroyed in the process,
as water is destroyed when it becomes air. In sequences of type (a), the
matter passes through different stages, each one realizing the potential
of the previous stage and each previous stage being a specific potential
for the next stage. In the process, the potential of each stage is used
up as it passes to the next until ultimately it realizes its nature fully by
becoming a man. There is a matter at each stage of the process, but
there cannot be a process unless there is a first matter from which it
begins. Hence, there must be a first material cause in sequences of this
sort. In sequences of type (b), the material at each stage is destroyed
as it passes to the next. All matter would eventually be exhausted –
which is impossible if the world is eternal – unless the process can be
somehow reversed. Hence, there must be a path, direct or indirect,
from air back to water. The crucial assumption here and throughout
book α is that it is impossible to go through an infinity. If an infinite
number of things have to happen before air can become water, it
never does become water. It follows that there must be a finite number
of steps in this process. Hence, there are a finite number of material
causes. There is, then, always a first step, that is, a first material cause,
of any process, though it may not be the same first.

A sequence of final causes without an end would be a sequence
without the Good. Moreover, if everything is for the sake of
something else, there is never anything that is good in itself and
therefore never any basis for action. Again, if there are an infinite
number of ends, each for the sake of another, there is no ultimate
end and, thus, no basis for action. Hence, there must be a "first"
final cause, the final cause that is the ultimate end of a sequence.

The formal cause of a thing is its essence. If there is an infinite
sequence, one formal cause would be known through another, and
so on. There would never be knowledge because every form would
depend on something else, and it is impossible to go through an
infinity.

For the same reason there would not be knowledge if the *kinds*
of causes were infinite (rather than four): it would be impossible
to go through all of them. The assumption here is that there is
knowledge (e.g. of mathematics and housebuilding). There could
not be knowledge if there were an infinity of causes. Hence, the
causes cannot be infinite.

If the causes are not infinite, there must be first causes. Again, this is not to say that there is some one first cause or even a single kind of first cause. Aristotle's point is only that each causal sequence must terminate in some cause, not that they all terminate in the same cause. Even so, the conclusion that there are first causes is very important: since metaphysics is the science of first causes, and since there are first causes, there can be a metaphysics. Moreover, the treatment of the causes in *Metaphysics* A and α is exactly the sort of treatment of all beings that metaphysics is to undertake. Thus, these two books not only argue for the existence of metaphysics, but, since they are themselves treatments of all beings, they are de facto evidence that there is a metaphysics.

Question for reflection:

1 What special properties must a thing have to terminate a causal sequence? In other words, how could there be a cause that is itself uncaused?

Book B: The Aporiai

The term *"aporia"* means "lack of passage," and Aristotle uses it to refer to a blockage of thought. Thought is blocked when there are equally powerful arguments for contrary conclusions. An *aporia* is, thus, an antinomy, a contradiction. All of *Metaphysics* book B is devoted to setting out the *aporiai* that are pertinent to metaphysics. Setting out the arguments that generate the *aporiai* that are intrinsic to a subject and resolving them is a part of Aristotle's philosophical method. Hence, there is no reason to think these *aporiai* are problems that Aristotle could not resolve for himself. As he explains, one needs to work through the *aporiai* of a subject in order to know the direction of inquiry and its end and to be able to judge between different doctrines.

How does Aristotle use the *aporiai* to advance his inquiry? Thought cannot rest in a contradiction. The purpose of setting out the arguments that generate an *aporia* is to discover the assumptions at work in these arguments. If there is some basis to reject an assumption that plays an important role in arguments for *one* side of the *aporia*, then Aristotle can remove the contradiction simply by rejecting or modifying the assumption. In this case, though, the antinomy is relatively easy to resolve and is not really intrinsic to the subject. The more important case is when the antinomy results from assumptions that seem undeniable, particularly when these assumptions are so embedded within the subject that they play a role in generating *both* sides of the *aporia*. An assumption that generates a contradiction must be rejected. If, though, the assumption is necessary for the science or, in our case, for *any* science, it cannot be rejected. Aristotle can only hope to modify it in such a way that it does not generate a contradiction but is still able to play its essential role. A modified assumption that meets these constraints is very likely to be true. If the modification is the only way to avoid contradiction, the modified assumption must be true. In this way, Aristotle can use *aporiai* to argue for new doctrines. The doctrine must be true if it resolves an *aporia* that, without it, would remain unresolved. Hence, setting out *aporiai* is part of a method for supporting new doctrines.

After brief remarks about the importance and use of *aporiai*, B.1 lists the *aporiai*. The rest of book B, chapters 2 through 6, expounds each *aporia* in turn by setting out the arguments on both sides. Issues that are mentioned in B.1 are not expounded in B.2–6, and an *aporia* set out in the latter does not appear in the former. In numbering the *aporiai*, I follow their order in the fuller account, B.2–6.

One or many sciences

Although book B does nothing more than set out the *aporiai* by expounding the arguments on both sides, a perceptive reader can see that the *aporiai* fall neatly into three groups. The first group, one to five, ask whether one or many sciences treat some topic, such as all four causes, the principles of demonstration, all the substances, all the *per se* attributes, and immaterial substances. Metaphysics is the science of the highest causes, the causes of *all things*. If all things cannot be treated by one science, there cannot be a metaphysics. We know from books A and α that there is a metaphysics (because there are first causes as well as an inquiry into them). Hence, all the topics must be included in one science. On the other hand, Aristotle has a precise idea of the structure of a science, and there are good reasons to deny that the topics metaphysics must treat can fall under one science. As we saw in the first chapter, he thinks that one science treats one genus. But the topics that metaphysics must treat do not appear to fall under one genus. In particular, (1) the four causes do not all belong to one genus because that would mean that each object in the genus, each being, would have all four causes, whereas only what is in motion has final and efficient causes and mathematical entities are not in motion. (2) The principles of demonstration (such as the principle of non-contradiction) do not belong to any one genus more than to any other. (3) If all the different substances belonged to a single genus, the science treating this genus would demonstrate all of their essential attributes, but in this case there would be no other science besides metaphysics. (4) If, on the other hand, all the attributes were included in metaphysics as instances of the genus that is its subject, then the same science will treat these attributes as both subjects and attributes. For example, a mathematical solid is both an essential attribute of a physical substance and a being in its own right. If metaphysics included all the attributes in its subject genus, then mathematical solids would be among its subject, but also demonstrated as attributes. Since the subject genus is assumed to be substances, metaphysics would be demonstrating substances; but it is impossible to derive one substance from another because substances are independent and self-subsisting. (5) If these mathematicals constitute a genus that is distinct from the genus which includes physical substances, as some Platonists suppose, then these thinkers are, again, doubling the universe in order to know it, but the sensibles remain unknowable and all the kinds of beings are not included in a single genus.

The key assumption in this first set of *aporiai* is that one science treats one genus. Although we have good grounds for thinking that there is a metaphysics, the topics it must treat do not fall within one genus. We will see later that Aristotle expands the notion of a genus and introduces other important doctrines to avoid these *aporiai*.

One principle

The second set of *aporiai*, six through nine, turn on the unity of the principle (or cause) of sensible substances. The principle is a constituent part of the substance. Only something that is one could be a principle or cause, for anything that is multiple has, as a prior principle, something one. However, there are different and seemingly incompatible types of unity that a principle should have. All the *aporiai* in this group arise because there are arguments to be made for each type of unity. Even those *aporiai* that seem to be about other issues, such as separation, are based on arguments for different sorts of unity.

It might seem that the easy way to skirt these *aporiai* is to reject the assumption that the principle is one. Aristotle does not do this or even consider it. Instead, he focuses on determining which type of unity a principle should have. Since different parts of a sensible substance have different types of unity, to ask about the pertinent type of unity is a way of asking which part is most important for the substance. Thus, one *aporia* posed here (6) is whether a substance's principle is a primary constituent of the composite or a primary constituent of its formula, such as its genus. Examples of the former primary constituents include a letter in a syllable, an elementary mathematical proof that is used in constructing more complex proofs, material elements such as fire and water, and a part of an artifact. Each of these examples is "one in number" because it is indivisible or, at least, not divisible into something else that is a primary constituent. On the other hand, a genus is one because it is an indivisible constituent of the definition. Since something is known through its definition, the genus is a principle of knowledge. Hence, the issue here is which of these two ways of being one qualifies something to be a principle. A case can be made for both. Apparently, Platonists proposed that the genus is a principle as both a constituent part and a principle of definition, but a part of a formula is not a constituent part of the thing defined (998b11–14). (7) The next *aporia* asks whether the principle is (a) the highest genus, that is, a categorial genus that is indivisible because it has no formula or (b) the lowest species which is indivisible in formula. The highest genus is one because it cannot be defined by differentiating some higher genus because there is no higher genus; in contrast, the lowest genus, that is, the lowest species is "one in formula" because its formula cannot be divided into another formula through which the same object can be known. *Aporia* (8) asks whether or not the principle is separate from individuals. On the one hand, it must be separate to be known, for an infinity of individuals cannot be known. It must also be separate if it is to be one and a principle. On the other hand, if the principle is separate and the principle of all things, then all things of which it is the principle are one. Finally, (9) how is the principle one? If it were one in number, it would be an individual and neither knowable nor the principle of anything else. If it were one in formula, it could not account for anything that is numerically one.

The key assumption in this set of *aporiai* is that a principle must be one. The problem is that there are good reasons for its being one in distinct, incompatible ways. We will see that Aristotle finds a way to reinterpret the unity requirements so that they can be met.

The highest principle

The final set of *aporiai*, ten through fifteen, explore candidates for the highest cause. These, too, turn on the kind of unity that a first principle must have. Whereas the second set explored the principle of *sensible* substances, this final set explores candidates for the principle of *all* things. The principle of a sensible substance accounts for the particular nature of that substance and sustains this nature. However, sensible substances come to be and pass away: the principle of a sensible substance comes to be present in matter and it ceases to be in the matter when the substance is destroyed. Because the principles of sensible substances do not exist eternally in matter, they require some other principle that is eternal to account for their motion or coming into being. This other principle is the first principle of all things. It does not account for a sensible principle's nature. It accounts for the persistence of the sensible nature's motion or its species.

Book B does not explain why a principle of all things is necessary. Instead, it looks at various candidates for the highest principle. The first is (10) a form that differs from the sensible only in being eternal. The problem is how something eternal can be the principle of what comes to be. The second candidate is (11) One itself or Being itself. Here the problem is that there would be nothing besides these principles. (12) Numbers, lines, planes, and other mathematicals are more likely candidates because they delimit bodies, but they cannot account for motion. (13) Platonic forms seem to be the first principles because they are both one in number and one in form, but it is hard to see how they could cause anything else or impart motion and persistence. (14) Actuality would seem to be the first principle because potentiality is defined through it, but inasmuch as a potential either comes to be actualized or fails to be actualized, the potential must exist temporally earlier than the actuality. (15) A universal should be the first principle because it is an object of knowledge, but the existence of the individual is prior to the existence of a universal.

In short, each of these is a candidate for the first principle because it is one. However, none is able to account for the sensibles and, therefore, none of these can be the first principle. This is the *aporia*. Aristotle considers these candidates in turn in B.5–6.

Book B is not often studied. One reason is that Aristotle rarely refers to it explicitly later, even when he resolves these *aporiai*. The issues book B sets out are not addressed in the ways their formulations might lead us to expect. But, then, the point of book B is to tie thought in knots so that we are forced to think about the issues differently and to endorse new doctrines. We should, thus, *expect* the issues to be discussed quite differently when they come up subsequently. Even so, the first set of *aporiai* is resolved in book Γ in ways similar to their formulations in book B.

The arguments book B sets out are important because they clarify certain troublesome metaphysical assumptions. I have already mentioned the assumption that one science treats one genus, the consequence of which is that the subject matter of metaphysics must be a genus if metaphysics is to be a science. Aristotle argues that being, the presumptive subject matter of this science, is not a genus (998b19–27). The argument is that every genus can be divided into species by means of contrary characters, "differentiae," each of which define one species. Thus, the genus animal is divided into a species that has blood and another species that has no blood or, rather, has no red blood. The differentiae here, blooded and bloodless, are not animals, and in general a differentia is not an instance of the genus it differentiates. It follows that being cannot be a genus because there is nothing which is not a being to differentiate it into species.

This result makes the existence of a science of metaphysics problematic because in order to find the first principle of all things, the metaphysician needs to know all things. If metaphysics were like other sciences, the first principle would be the generic nature common to all beings (just as the principle of animals is the nature of animal possessed by each individual animal). If, though, all things are not a genus, they have no common nature. How, then, could they be known? And what is the principle of all beings if it is not a common nature?

These questions point to an important assumption that is at work in *aporiai* 9 and 15. Aristotle claims that knowledge is of the universal (1003a12–17). (Again, "knowledge" = "science," and there is a single science of a single genus.) If being were a genus, there would be knowledge of it as a universal. Since being is not a genus, it would seem that it could only be a group of individuals. An individual could be simple, like a letter, or it could be a composite like Socrates. If all individuals were simple, there would be no composite entities and, thus, little of what we recognize as beings, nor any knowledge common to all beings. If, alternatively, an individual is a composite of matter and form, then it is still (apparently) unknowable. One reason is that any material composite has an indefinite number of attributes – think of all its relations with other composites – and what is indefinite cannot be known. Another reason the material composite is unknowable is that it comes to be and ceases to be, whereas knowledge is always true (cf. Z.15.1039b20–1040a7). So, any claim made about the composite becomes false when the composite changes. Thus, if being is not a universal, it could not be known.

On the other hand, if being were a universal, something else would be prior to it. An individual is prior to a universal, because no universal is a substance, and a substance is assumed to be prior (1003a5–12; cf. 999b24–1000a4). In sum, what is prior in being (namely, the individual) is unknowable, and what is prior in knowledge (namely, the universal) is posterior in being. Again, a science of first principles seems to be impossible.

Yet, books A and α show that there is a science of first principles. The problem for Aristotle is to explain how there could be such a science. This requires a careful examination of what a science is and a refinement of Aristotle's own conception of science as he lays it out in the *Posterior Analytics*. In other words, it is Aristotle's own conception of the structure of science that seems to exclude the possibility of metaphysics. In contrast, Plato's conception of science allows for the existence of metaphysics. It is the highest science because it deals with the highest principle, the one itself.

However, one who knows this principle knows everything that is one, that is, she knows everything. So on Plato's view, there is a metaphysics, but it swallows up all the particular sciences.

To show that there is a metaphysics, Aristotle needs to show that it has its own subject matter that somehow includes all things but remains distinct from the subjects of the particular sciences. This subject cannot be a genus nor can it be a group of individuals. This question about how metaphysics can have a subject matter, which is explored in the first group of *aporiai*, remains distinct from the questions about the unity of metaphysics' principles that are explored in the second and third groups of *aporiai*. As I said in the previous chapter, Aristotle resolves these questions in different parts of the *Metaphysics*. In all his other sciences, the subject matter is known together with its principles. Only in metaphysics are these two treated separately.

The contrast with Plato is instructive. Plato thinks knowledge consists of grasping a form. The form is the entirety of the subject matter and also its principle. When Plato claims that form is one, he is identifying the subject of knowledge with its principle. Aristotle agrees that the subject and its principle are each one, but denies that they are one in the same way.

The existence of metaphysics: books Γ–Δ

The first sentence of book Γ is a bold and famous assertion: "There is a science which investigates being as being and the attributes that belong to this in virtue of its own nature." The science is clearly metaphysics, and Aristotle is asserting that it exists. This assertion seems surprising because the *aporiai* of the first group call into question the existence of metaphysics. To be sure, we have seen that there is good reason to think that it does exist, but Aristotle needs to answer the objections to its existence. He needs to explain how the topics this science treats can fall under one science. Since he has not yet done this, the assertion of the existence of the science is best understood as a conclusion that has yet to be argued. It affirms that objections can be answered. We need to look to the subsequent discussion for Aristotle's arguments for his conclusion.

The first sentence identifies our science, metaphysics, as the science that studies "being as being." "As being" in this phrase refers to the way that science studies being. Mathematics studies "being as quantity" because it studies the quantitative aspect of beings, but that is another way to say that it studies quantity. By analogy, we might suppose that if metaphysics studies "being as being," it studies all of being. However, it is then puzzling how metaphysics could also study "the attributes that belong to being in virtue of its own nature"; for (a) what is there besides all of being that could serve as its attributes? Moreover, (b) being does not have a nature (if it did, it would be a genus) because no character is common to all beings, and (c) being does not admit of attributes because attributes belong only to substances – there are no attributes of attributes (1007b2–4). For these and other reasons, many hold that to study "being as being" is to study substance as such. On this reading, metaphysics studies all beings because it studies all substances and all their attributes; for all beings are either substance or attributes of substances. However, an Aristotelian science studies a substance and its *essential* attributes. If metaphysics studies all substances and all their essential attributes, it will not study all beings because many attributes are not essential to any substance.

The issue is: does studying "being as being" mean studying being or studying substances primarily? In my view both of these traditional readings miss the point Aristotle is making. To study something "as being" is to study it through its being, that is, through its essential nature. To study being in this way is to study the nature of being, and Aristotle is asserting the conclusion that, despite arguments to the contrary, *being does, indeed, have a nature.* The science that studies being studies this nature and the attributes that belong to being in respect of it.

This, at least, is what Aristotle's language indicates. The obvious problem is how to answer the argument that since being is not a genus, there is no nature common to all beings. This is the problem we encountered in book B. We will see that here in book Γ Aristotle resolves the problem by reinterpreting "nature." What, then, supports the conclusion that metaphysics studies the nature of being? What is this nature?

Γ.1 addresses the first question. We know that there is an inquiry into principles and highest causes, an inquiry that Aristotle's predecessors pursued and that he recounts in books A and α. Aristotle claims "there must be some thing to which these [principles and causes] belong in virtue of its own nature." He reasons that just as his predecessors were seeking the elements of beings ("existing things") not accidentally, but "as being," so he must seek the principles and causes of being not accidentally, but as being. We can appreciate this reasoning by imagining a science that studies animals. It would seek the causes of animals, and these causes would not be accidental but belong to animals in respect of their nature *as animals*, that is, essentially. Thus, this science supposes that animals have a nature and seeks its causes. So, too, the science of the first principles and highest causes of all beings presupposes that those causes belong to some nature.

As I understand Γ.1, Aristotle assumes that there is a science of the highest causes of all beings and that every science treats some generic nature. It follows that there must be some generic nature of being, and our science seeks its cause. As explained in my first chapter, in a standard Aristotelian science, this nature or, rather, its essence would just be the cause. Here, Aristotle is focusing on nature as the subject of a science and, thus, the subject to which causes belong.

What, then, is this nature? Γ.2 opens with the claim that all beings are "related to some one nature." The Greek expression here is *pros hen*, literally, "relative to one." Aristotle explains that the one nature is "substance," and he describes the different relations that beings have to substance. The term "substance" in this passage is usually understood to be the categorial genus of substance, in contrast with other categorial genera like quality and quantity. However, the relations he describes here are not, for the most part, relations between instances of categorial genera. His emphasis is rather on the production, destruction, generation and negation of substance. "Substance" is more likely the nature that any being acquires, loses, and negates, in contrast with the being's other features. There is support for this understanding in Aristotle's claim later in the *Metaphysics* that substance is primary because we think we know even a quality or a quantity when we know what each is (Z.1.1028b2). He means that we know a quality or quantity when we know its *substance*. What is the substance of a quality? Minimally, it is the cause that makes it be. We cannot help asking what this cause is. Of course, we want to identify some particular character that a being possesses that makes it be, but being's nature is not a determinate character, and anyway our passage seems to be saying something quite different, something that seems at first entirely trivial or wildly implausible: Evidently, each thing is a being by virtue of its substance, that is, its nature. It is because every being has its own nature that all of them are beings. What, then, is the nature of being? Substance. Not a particular genus or a class of beings to the exclusion of others, but the substance that is the nature of each being. If this is right, then Aristotle's claim here seems trivially reflexive: the nature of being is to have a nature. It is having its own nature that makes something be. To study a being as being is to study that being insofar as it has an essential nature. To be sure, the essential natures that beings have differ widely, but what all beings have in common is just *that* they have essential natures. It is this common, though indeterminate character that allows all beings to be treated together in one science.

It is not trivial to claim that each being has its own nature. Plato, for example, denies that a sensible being has a character that persists in it (*Phaedo* 78c–e, 80a–b). Aristotle needs to argue the point, and we will see how shortly. In order to understand his argument, however, we need to realize that he does not explain what it means to study being as being or to study being in respect of its nature. He uses the phrase "being as being" as what mathematicians call a "placeholder." It is like the variable x: the variable allows us to designate something without identifying what nature it signifies. Support for this claim lies in the *Posterior Analytics*'s use of similar expressions. There Aristotle refers to investigating "triangle as triangle" as investigating what belongs to triangle *per se* (I.4). He is speaking about the triangle's essential nature and its essential attributes. One reason to speak of "triangle as triangle" or "being as being" is that these phrases refer to an essence without indicating what the essence is. Thus, "studies being as being" refers to studying the essence of being, *whatever that essence might turn out to be*. Again, the phrase is a "placeholder"; it is like a mathematical variable without a value. Because Aristotle has shown that there is a metaphysics and that every science treats some subject essence, he can assert that metaphysics's subject, being, has an essential nature. What is this nature? To say that it is "substance" is merely to designate the nature another way, for here "substance," too, is a placeholder, a way to designate the nature and to contrast it with its attributes without saying what that nature is.

Just saying that being has some sort of nature does not suffice to disable the arguments against the existence of metaphysics set out in the first group of *aporiai*. For that Aristotle needs to show how one science can treat the following subjects: all the causes, the principles of demonstration, all the substances, all their attributes, and supersensible substances. Γ.2–3 advances seven arguments; each concludes that there is *one* science of some topic. Since we know that there needs to be one science for metaphysics to *be*, to argue for one science is to argue for the existence of metaphysics. Hence, these seven arguments support the conclusion which the first line of Γ expresses, that metaphysics exists. They do so by introducing new doctrines, doctrines that must be true because they, and apparently they alone, remove contradictions.

The first argument (1003a32–b19) is the most important. In this passage Aristotle refines his assumption that one science treats one genus. Medicine is primarily concerned with health in a body, but it is also concerned with everything related to health, such as diet, climate, signs of health, and so forth. In other words, its subject is not merely health but everything that is *healthy*, and the latter includes all that is related to health, including what is detrimental to health. Health is a genus because the definition of health belongs in the same way to each body that has it. Healthy designates a larger class, but it, too, is a kind of genus because every healthy thing is related to the definition of health. In other words, "health" is said "*in respect of*" one definition; "healthy" is said "*in relation to*" one definition. The Greek expressions for these ways of naming are, respectively, *kath' hen* and *pros hen*. Aristotle is saying that both are genera; the former is a genus in the strict sense, and the latter is a genus in a looser sense. Since medicine treats what is healthy, a *pros hen* genus can be treated by one science. Hence, it is still the case that one science knows one genus, but now "genus" has been broadened. Aristotle is reasoning: since (a) one science can treat a *pros hen* genus, and (b) being is a *pros hen* genus, then (c) there can be one science that treats all of being.

The obvious question is, what is the evidence for (b)? We might have expected Aristotle to argue it. It is a very significant claim about being. Not only does he not argue for it, but he does not explain what substance is and how things are related to it. Recall, though, that Aristotle's task is not to show *that* there is a metaphysics but *how* there can be a metaphysics. If being is *pros hen*, then it can fall under one science and there can be a metaphysics. Moreover, since the science that treats a *pros hen* treats some nature and what is related to it, the science that treats the nature of being, substance, can treat all four of the causes if they are all related to this nature. Just as one diet can be a source of health for some people, but not for others, so, too, one cause is related to some substances, but not to others. Substances that move have final causes; immobile substances and mathematical quantities do not need final causes. Recall that book B's first *aporia* is that because not all causes belong to each being, all causes could not be included in a science that would treat a strict genus of being. However, the *pros hen* genus includes whatever is related to any instance of a nature. All the causes can be treated by the science that treats being as a *pros hen* genus because each cause is the cause of some substance (1003a33–b19).

Although this passage's stated conclusion is that all the causes are treated by one science, we knew in advance that metaphysics treats all the causes. What is new here is that metaphysics *can* treat all the causes if being is *pros hen*. Evidently, Aristotle is using the first *aporia* to delimit the nature of being. Being must have that character that allows the first *aporia* to be resolved, namely, it is a *pros hen*. The assumption that one science knows one genus seems to exclude a science of being and a science of all the causes. On the other hand, the same assumption excludes there being a metaphysics if being or the causes fall to many different sciences. So it plays a role in generating both sides of the first *aporia*; yet, it cannot be entirely rejected because it is fundamental to Aristotelian science. Once it is refined, the *aporia* dissolves.

Aristotle has very little to say about how being is a *pros hen*. That is not surprising. Since all he needs to dissolve the first *aporia* is that being is *pros hen*, he is not in a position to determine being further at this point. Let us note again that the nature to which all other beings are related, "substance," need not be the categorial genus of substance in order to resolve the *aporia*. The source of this *aporia* in book B was that efficient and final causes do not belong to mathematical entities and, thus, that not all causes belong to all beings, as they must if being is a strict genus. To resolve the *aporia*, mathematical entities, which belong to the category of quantity, need to be among the substances; that is, mathematicals need to have natures to which causes belong. The causes of mathematicals need not be the same sort of causes as the causes of other natures, for the science of being treats everything related to the nature of being (substance), and not all that is related to this nature belongs to all of its instances. Hence, all that we can say about the *pros hen* character of being is that to study being "as being" is to study it insofar as it has a nature, that is, as a kind of substance, and that every being can be so studied.

How can this science study the attributes that belong to this nature essentially when these attributes are themselves beings and, therefore, fall among the substances treated by the science? The answer is that they are studied *as attributes*. To illustrate, the color white has a nature, and to study white "as being" is to study it through this nature. However, this nature of white also comes to be and ceases to be in ways that are characteristic of it; white is also indivisible in respect of its nature and to be indivisible is to be one. Hence, essential attributes of white include its manner of generation and destruction as well as its unity. Apart from how some causes could belong to some beings and not others, the *pros hen* doctrine of being explains how the same being that has a nature can also be an attribute of another being. Again, what the *pros hen* character of being explains is how being can have attributes even though those attributes are themselves beings and do not belong to every being. The nature to which those attributes belong is the nature of being. This nature is not a particular character. Rather, the "nature" that is common to all beings is just this: to have a nature. The attributes, thus, belong to each being in respect of its having a nature. These are attributes like a being's unity in respect of its nature and its having acquired that nature.

Substances and attributes

The rest of Γ.2 is devoted to exploring this nature and explaining its attributes. The details are too complicated to work through here. However, a brief sketch will help to prepare for the next stage of the inquiry. Γ.2 contains five more arguments for different topics falling under a single science, and Γ.3 adds a sixth such argument. Since these are all topics that metaphysics needs to treat, showing that they can fall under one science counts as arguing for the existence of metaphysics.

The first two of these arguments show together that all the substances fall under metaphysics. First, being, though it is not a genus in the strict sense, is divided into species. If being has a nature, then these species also have their own natures, and the species are further divided (1003b19–22). All these natures fall under the science that knows being. Second, associated with each of these species is a unity proper to the species, and these different kinds of one are also included within the science of being (1003b22–1004a2). Each of these parts or species of being is the subject matter of a part of philosophy (1004a2–3). In this respect, the parts of philosophy are like the parts of mathematics. Just as there is a first part of mathematics that deals with what is most one (the unit), and subsequent parts dealing with lesser unities, so there is a first part of philosophy dealing with what is most one and lesser parts dealing with lesser unities (1004a2–9).

The point here, left for the reader to infer, is that since the first mathematical science does not swallow up the others and lead to a single science of mathematics, the first part of philosophy need not swallow up the others. Hence, all the substances can come under philosophy without there being a single demonstrative science of all attributes. The first mathematical science is presumably the science of what is one in all respects, that is, the unit, and collections of units, that is, numbers. Subsequent mathematical sciences deal with what is one in one respect (the line), two respects (the plane), and so on. Although numbers are the subject of the first mathematical science, they are used by subsequent mathematical sciences. Likewise, the first part of philosophy deals with being insofar as it has a nature, that is, with the nature of each being, in contrast with subsequent parts of philosophy that deal with being as moving or as quantity. The natures expounded in the first part are used in subsequent parts, just as numbers play a role in all mathematical sciences.

The last three arguments of Γ.2 show how metaphysics can treat the essential attributes that belong to being as being. Book B's objection to a science that treats *all* essential attributes is that some substances will be demonstrated. Aristotle probably means that the line or angle that is an essential attribute of a triangle and is, thus, demonstrated by a science of triangles is also, in its own right, a mathematical entity with its own nature and, thus, a substance. A science that included all substances and demonstrated all their essential attributes would treat lines and angles as substances but would also demonstrate them as attributes.

Aristotle's first argument addressing this *aporia* (1004a9–31) shows that each of the four types of contrariety is defined in terms of the unity that belongs to a being's nature. Thus, a privation is the absence of unity within a genus, a denial is simply the absence of the unity, a contrary is a plurality, and a relation is said in respect of any of these. Since all are defined through the unity of a being's nature, they are all treated by the science that treats this nature. The nature is treated by the science that treats all beings in respect of their natures, metaphysics. Hence, all types of contrariety come under this science.

Now, this nature is a being, and all that belongs to it in respect of its nature counts as its attributes. It follows that these attributes of being must be treated by metaphysics. This argument, the second here (1004a31–b25), indicates some attributes that metaphysics treats, but it does not explain how to avoid the consequence that some substances are demonstrated.

The final argument (1004b27–1005a18) claims that all the attributes can be traced back to one and many. Since, then, these two, one and many, are treated by metaphysics, and since each being's other attributes are traced back to them, all the other attributes are also treated by metaphysics. More important than this conclusion is that, in arriving at it, Aristotle has answered the fourth *aporia*. The essential attributes of being are themselves and, thus, in respect of their natures, treated by metaphysics as substances, but they are not also demonstrated by this science. Instead, the attributes are "traced back" to their principles. Metaphysics treats all beings and all their attributes, but it does not demonstrate the attributes. It traces them back to natures.

Γ.2 concludes by listing some of these attributes (1005a13–18). They are treated in book Δ.

Principle of non-contradiction

One *aporia* raised in book B, the second, is whether the principle of non-contradiction (PNC) and other principles of demonstration are treated in metaphysics. Aristotle argues in Γ.3 that they must be treated in metaphysics because they "hold good of everything that is" (1005a22–3) or, to render his words more literally, because they "belong to all beings," and do not belong exclusively to one genus. Since only metaphysics has all beings in its scope, it is the only science that could treat these principles.

This argument does not appear, however, to resolve the *aporia* because it does not disable the apparent consequence of including the principles in a single science that also knows all the causes, namely, that there is a single demonstrative science of all the attributes. I suggest that Aristotle avoids this consequence by treating the principles as truly *belonging* to all beings, that is, as their attributes. Then, they are like other attributes of beings: they fall under the science because they are led back to a unity, but they are not demonstrated, nor are they used, in metaphysics, to demonstrate other beings.

Can these principles really be attributes? We saw earlier that the causes are things. Some principles are causes, but the PNC is not a cause. So it is not a thing. Neither is it merely a verbal formula, for a formula need not have any significance for being. The principle asserts: (a) the same thing cannot belong and not belong to the same thing, at the same time, in the same way, etc. Equivalently, (b) the same thing cannot be qualified by opposites, the same way, etc. Another formulation is: (c) the same thing cannot be and not be at the same time, in the same way, etc. These formulae contain indefinite qualifications. Still, the formulae assert something important about beings, namely, that they have some attributes but not others. It is because they have a limited number of attributes that they can be known, for to know something is to grasp what attribute it has and that entails understanding what lacks this attribute. In the case of something that has and does not have the same attribute, to grasp the attribute that it has does not enable one to distinguish the thing from what lacks this attribute, for it also lacks the attribute. What, then, is there to know about the thing? Its having one attribute does not exclude its having any other. Everything qualified by opposites would be alike in having all attributes. There is nothing about the thing to be known. Thus, to say that a thing is not qualified by opposites is to indicate an important feature of the thing, just the feature that enables the thing to be known, namely, that it has some determinate character and lacks other characters. Aristotle says that the PNC must be true if there is to be any knowledge. It is used in all the sciences. Clearly, it is a principle of knowledge.

It is not obvious, though, that it and the other principles do belong to *all* beings. Heraclitus famously denies the PNC. Plato affirms the PNC, but he denies that it is possible to give an account of sensibles that is free from contradiction. He apparently thinks that the principle applies only to the forms and that, accordingly, they alone can be known. If, as Aristotle claims, the principle does hold of all things, then all things, including sensibles, can be known. So, Aristotle's extension of the principle represents the bold claim that sensibles can be known.

What is the basis for the extension? Ostensibly, Aristotle is arguing for the PNC in Γ.4–8. However, he acknowledges that there is nothing that is better known than the PNC and no demonstration that does not assume it. What, then, is gained by arguing for the PNC? Aristotle notes that all such demonstrations begin by assuming that a term signifies an essential nature. If the PNC must hold, and if the only way to show that it does is if there is an essential nature, there must be an essential nature. That is to say, there must be at least one such nature if the principle belongs to anything. This raises an obvious question: which beings have natures? There are two arguments to deny that the PNC applies to all beings. By disabling those arguments, Aristotle removes the reasons to deny that the PNC extends to all beings.

Let us look first at Aristotle's first arguments for the PNC. As I said, he starts by assuming that a term means something, that "man," for example, means two-footed animal (1006a18–34). This definition is the "being for a man," that is, the essential nature of man. If this is what man is, then not-man must be something *different*. To claim that man is not-man is, thus, to claim that one thing is something else, that is, that "man" signifies not one thing, but two. Again if "man" signifies one thing, its essential nature, then not-man will signify something else, and to claim that man is not-man is to make man two.

On the other hand, if man were somehow not-man, then, since not-man is the furthest removed from man and the most opposite to it, there could be no reason to deny that man were anything else. Hence, it would be all things and all predicates would belong to it. By the same reasoning all predicates would belong to everything, and each thing would be the same as every other.

In short, denying the PNC leads to absurdity: either one thing is two or all things are the same. It might be objected that someone who denies the principle of non-contradiction would not be bothered by finding himself in an absurdity. However, either consequence is antithetical to significant speech. If "man" refers equally to man and not-man, then nothing can be said of either. If all things have the same predicate, then everything can be said about everything.

Why would someone who denies the principle of non-contradiction be concerned about significant speech? He cannot deny the principle unless the words he uses have meanings. If all the words have the same meaning, it is as impossible to deny the principle as it is to assert it.

Significant speech in this argument occurs when a term signifies some single nature that can be defined. Understood in this way, significant speech is necessary for scientific or philosophical discourse, knowledge, and whatever else requires definitions. That a great deal of human interaction does not require speech that is significant in this sense is shown in the plays of Harold Pinter and argued in the work of Ludwig Wittgenstein. Aristotle emphasizes significant speech because it is necessary for knowledge. His point is that we need the PNC for knowledge.

The puzzle is that in order to argue for the PNC, he needs to assume significant speech, and that means assuming that there is some nature to which a word can refer. Why should we think that there are natures whose essential formulae define them? No one really denies the PNC, but it is hardly clear that there are essential natures. Thus, Aristotle's initial assumption is far more problematic than the conclusion he draws from it, the PNC.

This putative conclusion is, I think, really an assumption. The PNC must be true if there is to be scientific knowledge, and there is such knowledge. As I said, the issue is what needs to be assumed to show the PNC is true. The answer is significant speech, that is, language that refers to definitions and essences. Because these latter must exist if the PNC is to hold and because the PNC must hold, definitions and essences must exist.

We can better appreciate this conclusion if we understand it in conjunction with the opening chapters of book Γ. There being is shown to have a nature that belongs to each being. Even a non-being "*is* non-being," Aristotle claims (1003b10). His point is that since every thing is a being, the negation of something is also a being. It follows that, conversely, being is qualified by both the thing and its negation, that is, by contrary characters. If the nature of every thing were simply being, the PNC would not hold. This is why it is important for Aristotle to discuss the PNC. In order for this principle to hold, individual beings must have natures that are more determinate than simple being. Such natures distinguish one being from another. To distinguish something and its negation as distinct beings, we need a nature like that of man. Man and not-man are two; whereas being and not-being are one, namely, being. In discussing the PNC, Aristotle is effectively arguing for the existence of refined natures, for an essence of man over and above the essence of being.

Just what beings have such essences? This is tantamount to asking how far the PNC extends. In Γ.5 Aristotle disables two arguments that purport to show there are contradictions in sensible characters. One is Protagoras' argument that a single object appears one way to one person and differently to another. The supposed implication is that the object has contrary characters. In general, Aristotle thinks that the character that we perceive exists in the perceived object: the form that comes to be in our sense organ exists with matter in the object. However, he also recognizes that in illness or injury the sense organ distorts the form. Hence, the characters that belong to perceivers need not necessarily belong to the thing perceived. So it is not a contradiction in the object that one person perceives an object to have one form and someone else perceives it to have another. Hence, Protagoras' argument for denying that the sensible object has a nature will not stand. Moreover, even if the perceivers disagree on whether the object is, say, white or sweet, they need to recognize the nature of white or sweet to recognize the disagreement.

A second argument that is supposed to show that sensibles are contradictory derives from motion. If something that is white becomes black, it comes to manifest a contrary character. Even when it was white it must have had the black within it, for it does not acquire the black from something external. Hence, the object that changes contains contrary characters, in violation of the PNC. Aristotle disables this argument by distinguishing between actual and potential characteristics. The white object does have black within it, but only potentially. When this potential is realized, the object becomes black actually and, also, white potentially. There is no contradiction in being actually one character and potentially the contrary character. Not only does Aristotle disable this ground for denying the PNC of sensibles, but he makes clear that the argument for denying the PNC presumes that white and black each have their own nature. Thus, Aristotle argues that all beings are subject to the PNC by disabling the arguments to the contrary. To be subject to the PNC, a being needs to have an essential nature that can be defined. Because all beings are subject to the PNC, all beings have essential natures and definitions. Since a being is known through its own essence, every being can be known. This conclusion contrasts sharply with Plato's idea that only forms have natures and that sensibles are known through them. Aristotle has argued, in effect, that *each* being can be known through a nature that distinguishes it from other beings.

That all beings have their own natures is one of Aristotle's really important metaphysical conclusions. At the beginning of book Γ, he emphasizes the common character that all beings share, the character that makes it possible to treat them all in a single science. This character is substance. It is difficult to understand how it is common. I suggested that "substance" is not the categorial genus, but a placeholder for the nature of being, whatever that would be, and that this "nature," at least in the opening of book Γ, is not a character that falls within a categorial genus, like two-footed animal and five feet long. Rather, what makes something be is merely its having a nature. So the nature of being is just this: to have a nature. This is clearly a "nature" only in an extended sense of this term, but it is *the* common feature of all beings and in respect of it there can be a science of all beings, a metaphysics. There is a metaphysics because we can know *that* all beings can be known. To know being as being is to know it through its essential nature, substance. The discussion of the PNC shows that the essential natures of all beings *cannot* be the same. All beings *cannot* be known by the same definition. Each must have an essential nature that is more refined than the nature common to being, substance. To understand not only *that* being is a nature subject to a science, but also *what* this nature is, Aristotle must explore the natures of different beings. This task Aristotle undertakes in the central books, *Metaphysics* E–Θ.

Book Γ wrestles with the being of being in order to know *that* beings can be known. The reflexivity is not accidental. However, the process of reflection leads to the investigation of *what* being is that occupies the central books.

Questions for reflection:

1 Can a person who steadfastly denies the PNC be forced to acknowledge his mistake?
2 Does a logical principle like the PNC assert or presuppose anything about the nature of world?
3 What sort of entity is a logical principle?

The essential attributes: book Δ

Book Δ is often said to be a dictionary of terms that is not connected with the sequence of thought in the *Metaphysics*. It consists of discussions of some 30 terms in as many chapters. However, it is not a dictionary. It aims, in each case rather, to set out the different kinds of things that are called by the same term and to explain, at least to some degree, in what respect these things are called by the term. There are, thus, three components here: (1) the term, (2) the things called by the term, and (3) that in respect of which they are called by the term. In general a thing is called by a term in respect of the thing's essential nature (see *Cat.* 1). However, the groups of things called by the terms discussed in book Δ do not have essences. Instead, we need to think of the third component as a quasi-essence, a character or a formula that plays the role essence does in the particular sciences, the role of explaining why a group of things is called by a term.

Many of these terms discussed in this book have already emerged. They are terms that cut across the categorial lines. "Time" and "place" are terms discussed in a particular science, physics. "Cause," "principle," "one," and "genus" could be said of things in any categorial genus. We could call them transcategorials. Book Δ elaborates the different groups of things of which a term of the latter sort is said and the different characters in respect of which the same term is said of the same things.

There are multiple respects in which things are called by each term. In none of these discussions is there a single respect in which all the things called by a term are so-called nor is there a single character common to all the things called by the term. In lieu of a common character, some of these discussions identify different ways things are called by a term and then show how these ways are led back to some primary way or to some type of thing to which the term most properly belongs and from which it has been extended to the others. This primary sense serves to unify all the uses. In a standard Aristotelian science, essential attributes would be demonstrated from an essential nature. Here, attributes are not demonstrated but "led back" to something primary if possible, something that is itself associated with a thing's individual nature.

The first eight chapters set out the different ways that something is said to be a "cause," the ways a thing is said to be a "principle" and, likewise, the way a thing is called, "element," "nature," "necessary," "one," "being," and "substance." Two of these chapters, those on "one" and "being," form the basis for extended discussions of things called by these terms in books I and E–Θ. Here in book Δ Aristotle does not identify a primary sense for either of these.

Since the attributes described in the first eight chapters belong to every being in respect of its essential nature, they resemble attributes said to be *per se* in the first sense distinguished in the *Posterior Analytics* (I.4.73a34–37). These are attributes that are contained within a thing's essential nature, as line is contained in the definition of triangle. The remaining attributes of book Δ belong to some beings, something like the way odd belongs to some numbers, as instances of what is said to be *per se* in the second sense of the *Posterior Analytics* (73a37–b3). In this case, the essential nature of the attribute includes that of the substance within it, in the way that the definition of odd includes number. Apart from the discussions of being and one, most of this material is not used later, but it is interesting in its own right.

Things are called "beings" accidentally if they are conjunctions. Things are called "beings" essentially if they are (1) in one of the categorial genera, (2) true rather than false, or (3) potential or actual. Aristotle elaborates on these ways of being in books E–Θ. Things are called "one" accidentally if they are conjunctions, and essentially if they are (1) continuous, (2) material or generic substrata (they are one because they are forms of, say, water, or instances of, say, animals), (3) indivisible in formula, (4) whole. Aristotle elaborates on the ways of being one in book I.

Book Γ addresses what the *Posterior Analytics* (II.1–2) calls the "is it?" question of scientific inquiry. It asks whether being is, which is to ask whether there is some nature through which being can be known. The answer is that being is known through a nature, the nature of substance. Although Aristotle does not identify substance here, I argued that each being is a substance insofar as it has a nature, and we saw that this nature cannot be common to all beings. There are attributes that belong to a being in respect of its having a nature. It must be and be one. It must be a cause. It is prior or posterior to other beings. It is complete or defective. In short, the attributes sketched in book Δ belong to a being by virtue of its nature. Insofar as being has a nature and attributes, there is a science of it. To pursue this science further, we need to understand what the nature of being is and this, we will see, requires finding what the primary being is.

What is being?

Having shown that metaphysics exists by showing that its subject matter exists, Aristotle turns to the next question, what is that subject matter? That is, what is being? The discussion begins in the first chapter of book E. Because Aristotle speaks here about finding the causes and principles of "being as being," this chapter is generally taken to resemble Γ.1–2. The text distinguishes the science that treats "being simply or *qua* being" from the sciences that study "some particular being – some genus," a distinction that Γ also makes. However, the central claim here in E.1 is that the particular sciences do not demonstrate the *essence* of the genus they treat. They make it clear by sensation or they assume it by hypothesis and, then, demonstrate through it the attributes that belong to the genus. Nor, Aristotle adds, do they consider whether or not the genus exists because "it belongs to the same line of thought to show what it is and that it is" (1025b10–18).

Aristotle clearly has in mind the two scientific questions of *Posterior Analytics* II.1–2, a topic I discussed in Chapter 1. His point here is that in the particular sciences they are answered together once we have the essence: we know *that* there is a genus when we know *what* it is, that is, when we grasp its essence. The particular sciences grasp an essence by sensing it (as when we see that a natural substance moves by itself) or by hypothesizing it ("let a triangle be a three-sided closed plane figure"). E.1 is contrasting these particular sciences with metaphysics. Metaphysics does not deal with a part of being, nor does it sense or hypothesize an essence. We saw that books B and Γ argue *that* there is a genus of being, that is, a *pros hen* genus of being, by showing that all beings can be treated by one science. These arguments do not show *what* the essence of this genus is. To be sure, book Γ does show that there is a nature of being, namely, substance; but it does not show what this substance is, and indeed substance here is not a single character. Hence, metaphysics is unlike the particular sciences in that the same thought does *not* show *that* there is a genus of being and *what* it is. It remains for Aristotle to address the second scientific question, "What is being?" This is the issue examined in the central books, E–Θ.

The reason these two issues are distinct in metaphysics is easy to see. In the particular sciences, we know that a genus exists when we grasp the essential nature that belongs to each of its instances. There is no such essential nature of being; what we grasp first is a sort of quasinature common to all beings, and we grasp its existence indirectly. There is a science of all beings because each being must have a nature. However, what we need to understand are the primary beings upon which these natures depend, those beings that have natures not through other beings, but through themselves. Whereas book Γ seeks what is common to being, the central books seek what is primary.

The difference in perspective between Γ and the central books has long troubled scholars, and some have even supposed them to be incompatible and to stem from different periods of Aristotle's development. However, we can see that the two perspectives are necessarily distinct parts of the same inquiry into being.

Since the inquiry into the nature of being seeks primary being, it is no surprise that E.1 turns immediately to the question of which essential natures are separate. (A primary being must be separate because anything that is not separate depends on what it is not separated from.) There are three theoretical sciences, Aristotle explains: mathematics, physics, and metaphysics. The objects of mathematics are immobile but they are not separate from matter, though mathematicians treat them as if they were separate. The objects of physics are mobile, and they, too, are not separate from matter. The objects of metaphysics are immobile and separate from matter. Hence, it is the first science.

Aristotle explains that some of what are defined are like snub and some are like concave. Snub is a concavity in a nose; it is understood as a form (concavity) in a matter (nose). The concave, however, is a form that is defined without matter. The objects of physics are like snub; they need to be defined with matter because matter is a principle of motion. The objects of mathematics are like concave; they do not have matter in their definitions because they do not move. However, concavity does not exist separately. It exists in matter. As I said, only objects that exist separately from matter can be primary because only such objects can be independent of everything else, whereas objects with matter must be dualities of matter and form and, thus, dependent on other things. Hence, if there are objects without matter, objects that are truly separate, they will be prior, and they will be the objects of metaphysics. Aristotle famously adds, the science of such objects will be prior (to other sciences) and "universal because it is primary," "and it will belong to this [science] to consider being *qua* being [being as being] – both what it is and the attributes that belong to it *qua* being" (1026a27–32).

He means to say that a science that treats form without matter is prior to a science that treats forms with matter and to a science that treats forms as if they were not in matter. Presumably such a science is universal because its conclusions about form apply somehow to forms that exist with matter, in something of the way that the conclusions of "universal mathematics" hold of all branches of mathematics.

Questions for reflection:

1 How could Aristotle prove the subject matter of metaphysics exists before he knows what it is?
2 Why is the "what is it?" question an inquiry into primary being, whereas the "is it?" question asks about the totality of being?

Aristotle's strategy

"Being" is said in many ways, Aristotle claims in Δ.7. That is to say, things are called by the name "beings" in respect of distinct sorts of characters. (1) Accidents, like the musical Socrates, are said to be; (2) instances of the categorial genera (that is, the most universal genera: substance, quality, quantity, relation, etc.) are said to be; (3) an assertion of truth as well as the thing asserted to be true are said to be, and a denial as well as the thing denied are said not to be; (4) what is actual is, while what is potential is, as well, but differently. The first way of being is accidental, the last three are *per se*. These three *per se* ways of being are not distinct slices of one pie. Instead, each way covers the whole pie. Some of the same things are said to be in all three *per se* ways.

Since there are four ways of being, the question, "what is being?" divides into four: what is accidental being? what is categorial being? what is actual or potential being? what is true and false? These four questions are treated, respectively, (1) in book E.2–3, (2) books Z–H, (3) book Θ.1–9, and (4) books E.4 and Θ.10.

It is important to understand what Aristotle is looking for. There is no essential nature common to all things called "beings" in *any* of the four ways, that is, no essence common to categorial beings, no essence common to actualities and potentialities, nor is there an essence common to what is true. Yet, if there were nothing at all common to things that fall under these four heads, there would be no nature of being. Although no nature is shared by all, there is a nature upon which all beings depend. Or, rather, *if* there is such a nature, then all beings will be known through it and have their own essential natures in respect of it. In other words, even in the absence of a nature that is common to all beings, metaphysics can come to know what being is by finding the principle upon which beings depend. This principle is the primary being through which or in relation to which the other beings are understood. Since there are many ways "being" is said, Aristotle must find the thing that is primary in respect of each way of being. We would then expect him to consider which among these four primary things is that upon which the others depend. However, we will see that there is a remarkable convergence among the primary things so that a single being is primary in all four ways. This being is, however, separate only in a way. Hence, it requires a still higher being.

Accidental being: E.2–3

What is accidental being? An accidental being is a conjunction of a substance and an accident or a conjunction of two accidents that belong to the same substance. Aristotle claims that there is no knowledge of accidental beings. One reason is that there are an infinite number of accidents and an infinity cannot be known. Thus, when a carpenter makes a house, he also makes something that is, say, pleasant to some, situated next to a tree, existing on someone's eighteenth birthday. Since this house stands in relation to every other being, past and future, its attributes are infinite. Another argument is that accidents are not the regular consequence of a principle. In general, events that occur from some principle are regular. Thus, since it is hot in summer and cold in the winter, a cold day in summer is accidental. It does not follow from the same principle. What occurs always or for the most part can be known, but what is accidental is not always or for the most part. Hence, what is accidental cannot be known. Further, what comes to be through an art like shipbuilding, comes gradually through a determinate process that depends on the art and on the material it works on. What is accidental exists without the pertinent process. Thus, anyone who builds a ship follows the determinate process dictated by the art of shipbuilding. It is an accident if a doctor builds the ship because the art of medicine does not dictate the process of building the ship, nor does the art of shipbuilding dictate that a ship would be built by a doctor. Hence, this accident cannot be known by either branch of knowledge (shipbuilding or medicine), nor by any other.

This idea of a character that does not come to be through a pertinent process lies at the heart of Aristotle's most famous example of the accidental. A man eats spicy food and goes to a well to drink water. At the well, he meets ruffians who kill him. Here, spicy food seems to be the cause of his death. However, eating spicy food would not ordinarily lead to a person's death. His being killed at the well is, as it were, a kind of attribute that he acquired without undergoing the process through which he would ordinarily come to possess it. There are multiple causes at work: eating spicy food causes thirst, which in turn causes a trip to the well, whereas something entirely different causes the ruffians to gather at the well. One cause leads to an expected result, the man's going to the well; another cause leads to an entirely different result. The plurality of causes that bring about the event cannot be known with a single knowledge because they belong to distinct arts or sequences. Insofar as there are multiple causal principles in the world, accidents are inevitable, and some portion of nature must remain unknown.

Questions for reflection:

1 Why does modern (Newtonian) physics reject accidents? Why do many medieval philosophers reject accidents?

2 Why does Aristotle think that some causes produce their effects only "for the most part"?

3 The phrase "accidental cause" would seem to be a contradiction. Why does Aristotle think it is not?

4 Are indeterminacy and other phenomena of quantum physics accidental causes?

Truth in thought and words: E.4

Aristotle's first treatment of being as true appears in E.4. An affirmation is true when the things it combines are combined; a denial is true when the things it separates are separated. So understood, true and false belong to thought or statements, not to things. Hence, Aristotle dismisses truth as an attribute of thought rather than a kind of being.

The truth of thought and statements is closely akin to accidental being. Musical Socrates is an accidental being. "Socrates is musical" is true. Indeed, Aristotle compares truth's causes to accidental causes, and dismisses both truth and accidental being (1027b34–1028a2).

What is puzzling, then, is why Δ.7 counts truth as a *per se* way of being and not as an accidental being. The answer must be that E.4 treats only a part of truth, the accidental part. For most of the chapter, Aristotle speaks as though he were discussing the whole subject, but at one point he proposes to leave the simple and the "what is it" for later consideration (1027b28–29). These topics, along with necessary and impossible conjunctions of things, belong to the treatment of the truth of things that appears in Θ.10.

The placement of these chapters is entirely appropriate: E.4 appears immediately after the account of accidental being because both are dismissed. Θ.10 appears after Aristotle's treatments of categorial being and being as actuality because it draws upon them.

Categorial being: books Z–H

One way of being is the categorial genera. That is, a thing is called a "being" if it is an instance of one of these genera. Aristotle's treatment of categorial being in Z–H is one of the most important, most difficult, and the least understood portions of the *Metaphysics*. As usual Aristotle gives readers few indications of the structure of the discussion. Yet, once we see this structure, the arguments and conclusions fall into place nicely.

Aristotle sets out the categories in a work titled *Categories*, a work that belongs to his logic. A category is a predicate that marks out the most general class of things sharing a common nature. Socrates, for example, is a man, and all men are mammals; mammals are animals, and animals are substances. Substance is the highest predicate of Socrates that designates a class with a common nature. All substances are self-subsistent entities (that is, they are not predicated of something else). "Being" is also predicated of Socrates, but there is no nature common to all beings. Likewise the most general predicates of white and 3 that mark out classes with common natures are, respectively, quality and quantity. What is important for the *Metaphysics* is that these categories constitute distinct genera of being (1016b31–34). The primary categorial genus is the one upon which all the other genera depend. This is substance. The initial understanding of substance is simply as those entities in which all the other beings can inhere. Here in Z.1, Aristotle claims that substance is prior to the other categories in formula, knowledge, and time (1028a31–b2). The essential formula of an instance of any other categorial genus includes that of substance.

This last claim is an important affirmation of what we saw in book Γ: all beings have essential natures. Moreover, the priority that Aristotle does ascribe to the category of substance in Z.1 is the priority that most readers have supposed him to ascribe to substance in Γ.2. However, Z.1 aims to show, not the unity of all beings, but the priority of the nature of substance to the natures of all being. If the formulae of all other beings are understood through the formula of substance, then to know what being is, it is crucial to know what substance is. Hence, Aristotle claims at the very end of Z.1 that the question "What is being?" reduces to the question "What is substance?" It is this latter that the rest of Z–H explores.

Aristotle's exploration begins by setting out, in Z.2, what are agreed to be substances. The best examples are animals, plants, their parts, and natural bodies, that is, earth, air, fire, and water. Disputed examples include mathematical entities, Plato's forms, and form numbers. In respect of what are these entities called "substances"? Z.3 sets out four possible answers to this question: essence, universal, genus, and substratum. The assumption here is that if A is the cause in respect of which something is a substance, then A is itself a substance in a higher degree (cf. α.1.993b24–27). It is important to understand that each of these four counts as an A. The issue here is which of these four is the *primary* respect in which the agreed-upon substances are called "substances."

Substratum

The rest of Z–H explores these four candidates. One of them, substratum, turns out to be three, and Z.3 distinguishes three substrata: matter, form (shape), and composite. The chapter goes on to argue against the material substratum's being the *primary* respect in which something is called a substance. The reason is that if something were a substance because of its matter, then the deepest matter, the matter that is without any characteristics or even position of its own, would be substance most of all. But a substance is a separate self-subsistent entity. So something without any character or determinate features could not be a substance. It could not occupy a place, have a boundary, be known or be anything at all.

This argument does not dispute that things are substances in respect of their material substrata. The point is rather that if being a material substratum is the primary cause of something's being a substance, then the *deepest* material substratum is its *highest* cause and is itself a substance most of all. It follows that form is a better candidate for primary substance than matter. The third substratum, the composite of form and matter, depends on the treatment of form. Hence, Aristotle puts off its discussion here and does not take it up again until book H.

Question for reflection:

What kinds of things are called "substances" in respect of their material substrata?

The logical treatment of essence: Z.4–6

We expect Aristotle to turn to the second type of substratum, form, but Z.4 considers another candidate, essence, and this discussion concludes in Z.12. However, in Z.6 Aristotle argues that essence is form. In Z.13–16 Aristotle argues that neither genus nor any other universal is a primary substance. It is clear that only essence/ form could be the primary substance. Z.17 explains how it can cause something to be a substance: it is the cause of unity among the material elements. Book H explores the remaining candidate, the third substratum, the composite. It needs to explain how the material elements and the form/essence are united in the composite. To do so, it identifies form/essence as actuality.

With this sketch of the structure of Z–H, we can consider some details. Z.4–6 undertake a "logical" treatment of essence. The essence of something is what it is *per se*. The formula of a thing's essence thus expresses what it is. There are two ways in which a formula can fail to express something's essence, by addition and not by addition. One could try to define musical by including the formula of man. This is a failure by addition. Or one could try to define musical man by defining musical. This is a formula that fails to make an addition. At first glance, these examples seem to be the mistakes of an incompetent definer, but they signal deeper problems. Musical does not exist apart from man or some other substance. Hence, to define musical it is necessary to add some substance or, at least, its dependence on substance. A definition of musical must, then, *inevitably* fail by addition. Likewise, the essential nature of musical man is the essential nature of man, for musical is accidental to man. Hence, an attempt to define the composite of substance and accident will necessarily fail to make an addition. The conclusion is that it is impossible to define an accidental attribute or a composite of substance and accidental attribute in such a way that the definition belongs to it and only it *per se*. The only entities that can be defined in this way are substances. Since a definition is a formula of an essence, only a substance has an essence.

Yet, in the process of showing that accidents and composites do not have formulae that belong *per se*, Aristotle explains, at the end of Z.4, that they do have formulae that, by the "addition and subtraction" of substance, define them in a secondary way. (The Barnes translation renders this phrase "qualifications and abstractions.") But subtracting substance that is always present with an accident, we can define the accident in a secondary way; by adding substance back, we can define the composite. It follows that accidents and accidental composites do have essences in some secondary way. As Aristotle explains, essences belong to substances primarily, and in a lesser way to other beings.

Besides substances, composites, and accidents, there is another group of beings that have secondary essences, the essential attributes that are defined through a particular matter (Z.5). Aristotle's paradigm case is snub, a concavity that exists in a nose. Since nose is included in the definition of snub, and since the formula of concavity does not define snub, snub has no formula that expresses what it is *alone*. Aristotle argues by a reductio ad absurdum: if "snub" is concave nose, then "snub nose" would be concave nose nose, repeating nose. Since, moreover, a concave nose is a snub nose, "snub nose" could be substituted for the first two terms in "concave nose nose" yielding "snub nose nose." But "snub" is, again, concave nose, and this latter can again be substituted for "snub" yielding "concave nose nose nose," and so on ad infinitum.

Aristotle's point is that an essential attribute like snub includes within itself the substance to which it belongs so that attempting to define it risks an infinite regress of substances. So an essential attribute, like an accident, does not have an essence, except in a secondary way, namely, by the addition and subtraction of substance.

Z.6 argues that each thing is identical with its essence, provided that the thing is said *per se*. What does he mean by "each thing"?

The argument makes clear that the thing is that to which the essence belongs. This is generally assumed to be the individual substance, that is, the composite of matter and form. However the argument that we saw in Z.4–5 would apply here: if the formula of the composite does not express the nature of the matter, as it does not, it fails to add a part of the composite; whereas a formula that does include matter does not express the nature of the thing. If, then, the thing is that to which the formula belongs *per se*, the thing would have to be the form; for the formula expresses the nature of the form. It is this form that Aristotle is here equating with essence. To be sure, the essence and the composite are also the same, but only in a way; Aristotle returns to this identity at the end of book H.

That "each thing" in Z.6 is Z.3's second type of substratum, form, explains why Aristotle refers here to Platonic forms like good itself and animal itself, for these forms are identical with their essences.

Once we see that "each thing" is form, Z.6's arguments make sense. Suppose a form and its essence are distinct. Since the essence is what is known, the form remains unknowable. Moreover, an essence that is distinct from the thing whose essence it is would not be a being. Both are absurd. Hence, form is essence in whatever is said *per se*. As we saw in Z.4–5 only substances are said *per se*. So the form and essence of a substance are identical.

This reasoning does not apply to accidents and accidental composites. Is the essence of white man the same as that of which it is the essence, the thing that is the white man? Suppose that it is. We know that (1) man and white man are the same thing, and we have just seen that (2) man and the essence of man are identical. Assuming that (3) the thing white man is identical with the essence of white man, we must infer from (1) that man is identical with the essence of white man and, then, from (2) that the essence of man is identical with the essence of white man. This conclusion is at odds with Z.4's claim that white man has its own essence *by addition*. Furthermore, if the essence of white man were the essence of man, then the essence of musical man would also be the essence of man, and it would follow that the essence of musical is the essence of white. An absurdity. Hence, it is only substances whose form is their essence. The essences of other beings are either the essences of the substance in which an accident inheres or essences that are by addition.

In sum, in a substance, the essence is the form. Aristotle is identifying two candidates for primary substance. Form or essence would seem to be that in respect of which something, namely, the composite of form and matter, is primarily said to be substance. Yet, this form exists with matter. It is, first, acquired and lost by matter; second, it seems to be divided by a composite's material parts. Aristotle must show that form is not affected by the matter in which it exists. Only as such can form be the cause of the composite's being a substance. Thus far, Aristotle has treated essence "logically," that is, through the formula that expresses what it is. Z.7–11 consider it physically and materially.

The physical treatment of essence: Z.7–9

A sensible substance like a man or a plant comes to be. Does its form or essence also come to be when it comes to be? Or is it rather that a pre-existing form comes to be present in some pre-existing matter? Aristotle argues the latter. The reason is that whenever something comes to be, there is some matter from which it comes to be. If, then, the matter came to be when the composite is generated, there would be another matter and another form from which it came to be. We would need to ask the same question about that matter, does it come to be along with the composite or did it exist prior to the coming to be of the composite? Again, if it came to be, it was from still another matter, and so on, ad infinitum. To avoid regress, we must say that there is some matter that is not generated in the generation of the composite. There is no reason not to say that what exists prior to the generation of the composite is simply the composite's matter. The same reasoning applies to the form. If it is generated in the generation of the composite, it must come from a prior matter and form, which latter must, in turn, come from a still prior matter and form, and so on. To avoid regress, we need some form that is not generated, and there is no reason this form should not be the form of the composite. It follows that a composite is generated when a pre-existing form comes to be present in a pre-existing matter.

The obvious question is, where does this form exist before it comes to be present in the composite? It must exist in some other substance. Given that the agreed-upon substances are plants and animals, the form could only have existed in the parents or, at least, one parent before coming to be in the offspring. This means that the form that comes to be present in the offspring is the *same* form that exists in the parent. Hence, the form or essence of a substance is unchanged through generation. If form did change, it would require a prior principle. Hence, the process of generation is not a reason to say that a substance's form requires a prior principle to account for it. On the contrary, since the form serves as a principle of a substance's generation, there is good reason for taking the form to be the principle of the substance.

Something similar holds of attributes. A piece of brass becomes round because it is fashioned by an artisan. The form of round that exists in the artisan's mind comes to be present in the brass without change. However, the form in the mind is not an actual round object. Only in the case of substance does the form pre-exist in the same way as it exists after coming to be present and, therefore, remain entirely unchanged in the generation.

Aristotle's reasoning in this section excludes the idea that individuals in the same species have individual forms. Your form belongs to you and is present in your matter, but it must be the same form as your father's. It does not contain the matter from which the composite substance comes to be.

Essence and matter: Z.10–11

In general, any of a thing's parts are its matter. Are the formulae of these parts included in the formula of the whole thing? Sometimes. The formula of the semicircle is not a part of the formula of a circle, but the formulae of letters are parts of the formula of a syllable. The formula of an acute angle is not a part of the formula of a right angle; but the latter formula is part of the formula of the acute angle.

To understand Aristotle's examples, we must recall that he does not use "matter" to designate a particular entity, as the term now does, but to signify any constituent or part in respect of some whole or some nature. The matter Aristotle is inquiring into here, the matter that may or may not be part of the formula of the thing, includes: (a) that upon which the form is imposed and which remains when the form is not present, that is, the matter of the composite, as well as (b) that which is organized into the form, such as the letters of the syllable. The "thing" here is substance, but since, as Aristotle puts it, "substance" can indicate (1) matter, (2) form, and (3) the composite of the two, the parts (=matter) of the thing (substance) could be (a) the matter of the composite or (b) that from which the formula of the form is composed (1035a1–4). Some editors add another matter, (c) the parts of the matter (see Barnes's translation of 1035b31–33). This would be the matter of substance (1), that is, the matter of the "matter," a notion that does not make sense unless "matter" is some form or composite.

When a composite, that is, a concrete individual, ceases to be the substance it is, what remains is its matter. When, for example, a man dies, "the bones, muscles, and flesh," that is, the body, remains, though the man does not. This body could not have made him a man; if it did, the body would still be a man. It must have been the form that made him a man. Hence, though form and matter both pre-exist the composite, it is the form that, coming to be in the matter, makes it a substance. Indeed, Aristotle says that the matter is not properly the substance (1035a7–9).

It follows that the formula of the form is more properly the formula of a substance than the formula of the matter. There is a formula of the composite "by addition," that is, a formula constituted by combining the formula of the form with the formula of the matter. However, the formula of the form is prior to this formula of the composite because it is a constituent of the formula of the composite. Since the substance of a thing is that in respect of which the thing is a substance, and since it is form rather than matter that makes something a substance, the formula of the substance is most properly the formula of the form.

Although some parts of the composite individual persist after its destruction, they do not persist as they exist in the individual. Famously, Aristotle claims that a finger severed from a person ceases to be a finger. Evidently, the part acquires its nature from the whole and is posterior to it. On the other hand, the parts of the form, such as the letters of a syllable do belong to the formula of the form and, therefore, to the formula of the substance. Hence, the formulae of the parts of a composite are not parts of the formula of the substance, whereas the formulae of the parts of the form are parts of the formula of the substance.

There is an obvious problem: why stop removing material parts? If the matter of the composite does not belong to the formula of the substance, why should the matter of the form? Instead of defining the syllable as particular *letters* that are juxtaposed, the syllable should, it would seem, be defined as their *juxtaposition*. This latter would eliminate matter from the definition of a syllable. Similarly, we could eliminate other material from other forms. The semicircle belongs to the matter of the circle (because it exists in the circle potentially), and it is therefore not included in the formula of the circle's form. But why stop there? Instead of defining a line as a magnitude, which is clearly a material entity, it would seem better to define it through its form, two, and, likewise, instead of defining solids through their volume, it would seem better to define them in terms of their form, three. We can push this line of thought still further: the form of the two and three would be the one. It seems arbitrary to eliminate only physical matter from the essence when it is possible to eliminate all matter from it. Since parts are always material, a form without any parts, like the form of the one itself, has no matter at all.

This reasoning is clearly Platonic, but what is wrong with it? Aristotle's objection is that the higher the level of form, the more removed the definition is from the feature that is essential to animals, their movement (1036b28–32).

This claim is difficult to understand because (a) the animal's motion requires a *physical* matter that persists through change (see *Physics* I.7), whereas the inference Aristotle draws is that the form must contain parts. These parts are the *matter of the form*, not physical matter. Moreover, (b) the motion that defines an animal, like the capacity for a specific work that defines a hand, is a function; and a function does not have either formal or physical matter.

These two difficulties are easy to answer. The motions or functions that define an animal or a hand can only occur in a physical body, and the body needs to be structured so as to be able to perform its function. Not only must the body have structural parts (such as fingers and an opposing thumb), but the function must be performed by these parts. The hand, for example, grasps and releases. So the function *does* have formal parts, and it can exist because the body has material parts. Contrariwise, if all the form's parts were abstracted out so that form really were one and indivisible, like the one itself, it could not be present in matter but would be separate, like Plato's forms. A form separated from matter could not move.

Thus, by eliminating the physical matter from the form (Z.10) and, then, by eliminating those forms that are removed from functions (Z.11), Aristotle has explained a way in which the form of the composite, that is, the essence, can be substance. As he notes at the end of Z.11, the form does not include physical matter, but it exists in matter just as snub is a curvature in a nose and the soul is a functioning of a body. It is just this form that, the last lines of Z.11 claim, is identical with its essence, whereas composites of form and matter, composites of substance and accident are not identical with their essences, just as we saw in Z.6.

Since Z.1, Aristotle has been looking to answer the question, "what is substance?" However, the answer that it is essence scarcely seems helpful because the phrase that is translated as essence is literally "the what it is to be" (*to ti ēn einai*). In other words, Aristotle answers the "what is it?" question by saying it is the "what it is." This answer is hardly informative. It is a tautology. If, though, the "what it is" is form, and form is, somehow, function, Aristotle has made some progress in answering the question.

Unity of definition: Z.12

Since we now know that the formula of the essence of a thing includes the formulae of its formal parts, the obvious question is whether or, rather, how the various parts of a formula are unified. To judge from Z.11, the parts of the form are necessary for motion. Z.12 does not consider these parts, but the parts of a definition of form. The formula of a substance's form consists of two parts, a genus and a differentia. How can these two components constitute a single definition of a single form?

Aristotle proposes a simple, but far-reaching solution. First, he introduces the idea of proper differentiation. A genus should be differentiated by differentiae that are proper to it, that is, by qualities that belong to it alone. Since, for example, something is an instance of the genus animal by virtue of its power to move and to sense, the differentia of this genus should specify these powers further. Thus, some animals move on land with feet, others at sea with fins, and still others in the air. All animals have the capacity to move themselves, but some exercise this capacity by having feet, others by having fins, and still others by having wings. These differentiae divide the genus of animal into species, and these species, in turn, are genera that can be further differentiated. The genus of footed animals, for example, can be divided by specifying the number of feet. There are, thus, two-footed and four-footed animals. These latter are also further differentiated. Four-footed is a differentia that properly divides the genus "footed animal." Many other characters divide the genus animal. Having hair and having scales divide it, but neither is a further determination of the defining feature of the genus, the power of self-movement, in the way that four-footed is.

As long as a genus is differentiated properly at every division, the last division, the ultimate differentia will contain *all of its differentiae*. Once, say, four-footed is introduced, it is not necessary to add footed because this latter is contained in four-footed. Moreover, to be properly differentiated the genus must be divided by characters that belong to the genus alone. That means that once the last differentia is specified, this differentia contains not only all previous differentiae but the *genus* as well. The genus is the matter of the species (1038a5–8), and the ultimate differentia must be the form of the species. (This is a difficult point for Aristotle to express because he uses the same Greek term *eidos* to refer to both form and species.) It follows that, despite appearances, the genus–differentia formula for a definition does *not* contain a plurality of parts. Although the definition is a formula with two parts, both parts are contained implicitly within a single part, the ultimate differentia. Just as the parts of the formula turn out to be one, so too the parts of the form that they signify are also one. To repeat, the form or essence of a substance is its ultimate differentia because this implicitly includes all other differentiae and the genus. Hence, the form or essence of a substance is one. The material of this form, that is, the genus, does not make the form many, nor is it necessary to look for a principle that unifies the parts of the form.

Z.12's argument for the unity of form is often taken to be peripheral to the main thrust of the discussion. It would rather seem to be a capstone that puts the preceding discussion into perspective. The issue is whether it is in respect of its essence that something is a substance. An obvious objection is that non-substances have essences as well. Aristotle's response in Z.4–5 is that accidents, accidental composites, and essential attributes have *secondary* essences, essences by addition or not by addition. Only substances have essences that signify the thing alone. Indeed, not only does a substance have an essence, but, as we learn in Z.6, the substance *is* its essence. This thing, the substance that is its essence, is form. In other words, the form is essence. This is true only of substances. Accidents have essences, secondary essences, that signify more than just the thing; composites of substances and accidents have secondary essences that signify something less, namely, the form.

Z.7–9 argue that although the form exists with matter in the composite and although this composite comes to be and passes away, the form does not change. It is passed along from one matter to another. The matter of generation does not belong to the form. Z.10–11 distinguish the form or essence from the material constituents of a composite. These latter do not belong to the form and cannot, therefore, make it many. Finally, Z.12 shows that the formal parts of the form do not make it many. Throughout the discussion Aristotle is intent on showing how form or essence is one. It is one because it does not include matter and because its formal parts belong to a single part, the ultimate differentia. Form must be one to be the cause of substance. Were it a plurality, it would need some other cause to unify it, and something else would be the cause of substance. Even so, its unity is not absolute; being one does not exclude its having parts and, thus, some sort of matter. Z.4–12 is an argument for essence or form's being the primary substance, that is, that thing in respect of which the generally accepted sensible substances are called "substance."

Question for reflection:

1   Z.11 argues that a substantial form must contain matter if it is to account for the substance's motion, but Z.12 identifies a matter that is implicit within the differentia. Is the latter matter the matter that plays a role in motion? Insofar as Z.11 shows the need for a matter that is *distinct* from form and Z.12 the need for a matter *within* the form, are the two chapters consistent?

Genus and universal: Z.13–16

Aristotle treats genus and universal, the last two of Z.3's candidates for substance, together in Z.13–16. Since a genus is a universal, we might wonder what the difference between them is. The genera Aristotle is concerned with are the category of substance and the genera that fall under it; such as, animal, mammal, human being, and so forth. These are substances, but they are not primary. In the *Categories* Aristotle calls them "secondary substances." The universals Aristotle is concerned with are being and one. We know from book Γ that being is a kind of substance because it is a genus in a secondary sense, and we know from book B that it is not a genus in the strict sense. Many arguments in Z.13–16 apply to both candidates, though Z.14 specifically discusses the genus and Z.16 is concerned with the one.

A genus is a universal because it is a "one over many," that is, because it signifies one character that belongs to many instances. Man is a genus, as is animal, because each man or each animal has a character such as "rational animal" or "having the capacity to sense" that belongs to every man or animal. At first glance a thing's essential nature would seem to be a universal because the character that makes something be, say, a man is shared by all men. However, Z.13–16 argue emphatically that no universal is primary substance. Can "rational animal" be an example of the genus-differentia definition that Z.12 claims defines a single essence without being a universal?

Indeed, many readers are puzzled by Aristotle's distinction between universal and essence. We can understand the distinction from his arguments against universals. A universal is, by its own definition, *common* to many things. In contrast, the substance of each thing is what is *peculiar* to it, something that does not belong to another thing. If a thing's substance is also what something else is, the first thing must be the second, for "things whose substance is one and whose essence is one are themselves also one" (1028b9–15). Furthermore, a substance is not said of a substratum, but a universal always is (1038b15–16).

Evidently, since form or essence is not universal, it is not said of a substratum; rather, it must be a substratum. Recall that Z.3 included form among the substrata. The claim that a form is not a universal is hard to express in Greek because the term for form is *eidos*, a term that also signifies a species, and a species is a universal. However, the form that exists with matter in the composite is not the universal, but the particular form of that particular composite. Even though it is called by the same term as the species, this form is a particular, not a species. The rest of this section helps us appreciate the difference.

First, Z.14 supposes that the form of man is composed of the form animal and the form two-footed, a view he ascribes to Plato. Likewise, the form of horse will also have the form of animal as its constituent. Is the form of animal in man one and the same as the form of animal in horse or is it different? If it is the same, then the form animal will exist apart from itself in distinct individuals. If it is different, then there will be as many forms of animal as there are species or individuals, that is, an indefinite plurality. But the (Platonic) form is supposed to be the *one* nature common to many instances. Aristotle's conclusion is that one form cannot be composed of other forms. This is not the case with a universal: one universal can be composed of others; thus, the species man is composed of the genus animal and a differentia. Despite its similarity to the universal, Aristotle's own form man does not contain two constituents that each exist separately, for Z.12 argued that animal is implicitly contained within two-footed.

In Z.15 Aristotle argues that an individual is unknowable. First, the composite individual is unknowable because of its matter. A composite comes to be and ceases to be. Hence, claims about the state of an individual will eventually be falsified. But knowledge is always true. So the composite cannot be known. However, it also follows that there can be knowledge only of what does not come to be, for example, the matter and form from which a composite comes. Matter is unknowable as matter, but it can be known through its form as, for example, flesh and bones have their own forms even though they are the matter of a human being. Hence, it is possible to construct a formula of an individual composite by combining the formula of its form with the formula of its matter. However, such a formula is not merely the formula of an individual but of all instances of this form and this type of matter.

On the other hand, Plato and others claim that form is individual because it exists separately. Aristotle argues that neither can such an individual be defined because any definition will be universal. The formula of a Platonic form will also be a formula of instances of that form and, therefore, not merely the formula of an individual. Moreover, since, as we saw, Platonic forms are composed of other forms – for example, the form man is composed of animal and two-footed – a formula of man will also be a formula of animal and of two-footed. Perhaps, someone will object that an individual could be defined by the *conjunction* of universal terms; for example, the formula of man would be the formula *only* of what is *both* animal and two-footed. Even so, such a formula is universal and, thereby defines all that comes under it, even if there is only one thing, such as the form man, that does come under it.

In sum, Z.15 argues that the formula of a composite thing cannot define it because either it does not include matter or, if the formula does specify the form of matter, it would be universal and so not define the individual. On the other hand, a form (like Plato's) that is supposed to be individual cannot be defined because a formula of it would define other things. What cannot be defined cannot be known.

Aristotle does not say so, but his own form does not have these difficulties. We saw that, though it has a material constituent, a genus, this is contained within it and, thus, known through it. Further, Aristotle's form is not a conjunction of separately existing forms, but contains implicitly other, less determinate forms. So a formula of Aristotle's form would not also be the formula of a distinct constituent form. There are many men with the same Aristotelian form, and a formula of this form must also be a formula of all its instances, but only secondarily. The formula is most properly the formula of the form. This form is a distinct entity, an essence. It is defined and known through its essential formula.

Furthermore, it is clear that Aristotle's form is one in formula (namely, the ultimate differentia) and that Plato's form, insofar as it is composed of other forms, is not. If unity is a requirement for being a substance, then some of the things that Z.2 lists as agreed-upon substances turn out, after all, not to be substances. Thus, the opening lines of Z.16 claim that the parts of animals and the simple bodies are not properly substances because they do not exist separately or they are not each one, though they are potentially one. If, then, it is oneness that makes the other agreed-upon substances be or not be justly termed "substances," the one itself would seem to be that through which something is a substance. However, the one itself is a universal; if the substance of a thing belongs to that thing alone and if one is the substance of all things, then all things will be the same substance, an absurdity.

In short, Z.13–16 distinguish Aristotle's form from the universal. The form is the substance of one thing, but the universal belongs to many. The form has a formula that belongs only to it even if it has many instances, whereas the Platonic form shares a formula with its own parts. Since the form has no parts, it is one, whereas the Platonic form is a universal that contains other separate universals.

Question for reflection:

1 Does Aristotle succeed in distinguishing the universal from his own form? What features of his own form emerge in the discussion? What are form's relations to the composite and to the universal?

Form as cause of unity: Z.17

Z.17 argues that the form is the cause of unity in the composite. The argument is important. Suppose the substance consists of material parts. What is the difference between those material parts lying in a heap on the floor and the parts assembled into a substance? If the answer is some other material part, we can raise the same question, what is the difference between it lying in a heap with the other material parts and the assembled substance? To avoid regress, there must be some cause that is not material. This cause is the form. Hence, the form is the cause of unity in the composite because it unifies the material by ordering or organizing them.

With this argument, it is clear that form belongs to a composite and makes the matter be one and, thereby, a substance. A universal could not perform this function in the composite. The universal does not exist within the composite.

In short, the form or essence of a thing is its substance because it causes the thing to be what it is. It remains to be explained, however, how this form can be present with matter in the composite without making the composite a plurality. Further, it is unclear at this point what the form does in order to cause unity. We will see that Aristotle addresses both issues in book H.

The composite: book H

In Z.3 Aristotle mentioned the composite together with form and matter as substrata. Since the composite is composed of these two, it is posterior, and Aristotle put off its discussion. Book H is the discussion of the composite substratum, though it also discusses the two other substrata. It begins by summarizing the previous book, but Aristotle soon turns to the generally recognized sensible substances (1042a24–31). These are all sensible substances and, thus, have matter. The substratum is their matter, and it is the substance of these sensible substances in three ways: (1) it is their matter, which though "not a 'this' actually, is potentially a 'this'"; (2) it is the form, which is a "this" and is separate in respect of its formula; (3) it is the composite, which is absolutely separate. The form is less separate but more one than the composite. Book H considers each of these substrata.

At the end of H.1 Aristotle explains that there are different sorts of matter for different sorts of motions. Generation is one motion, local motion another. The matter of sub-lunar sensible composites is a matter for generation, whereas the matter of the heavenly spheres is a matter for local motion. We know from book Z that form or essence is the primary cause of substance in a composite, but the task here is to explain how the material substratum also makes a sensible composite a kind of substance.

Having discussed matter, Aristotle turns to the form. He begins with artifacts in H.2. The form is often an ordering or arrangement of the matter. The boards become a lintel when they are arranged in one way or a threshold when arranged differently; pages become a book when they are glued into place. Importantly, the arrangement or what binds is, first, a principle of unity insofar as disparate matter is unified by the glue and, second, what allows the book to be used. Aristotle speaks of the order or arrangement as the differentia that makes the substance what it is. He means that it is a particular arrangement that makes the boards a door lintel because when they are so arranged, the boards are able to function in a particular way. Boards and bricks lying in a heap are potentially a house. When the boards are nailed into a frame and a roof and the bricks arranged around it, they are actually a house.

A house and other artifacts can be defined in three ways, through the matter, through the form, or through both. The form is the structure of the house that enables it to perform its function, namely, providing shelter for men and possessions. The boards and bricks that are the matter can be put to other uses, and the function can sometimes be attained with other material. Hence, the most complete definition of the artifact mentions both form and matter. What Aristotle calls here the artifact's "differentia" makes the artifact one, but the artifact's matter does not lose its identity in the composite. Hence, the artifact remains a plurality. Since unity is a mark of being, the artifact is not a being in the strict sense. It follows that neither it nor its differentia is properly a substance, though it is analogous to substance (1043a2–7).

The analogy becomes clear in the final chapter of book H where Aristotle completes the treatment of the composite as a substratum. There, Aristotle asks what is the cause of the composite substance's unity? Thinking about Z.17 and H.2, we might expect him to answer that it is the form that unifies the matter. Instead, he claims that the form and the proximate matter are, in a way, one inasmuch as form is actuality and matter is potentiality (1045a17–23).

How are actuality and potentiality one? Why is their unity any less problematic than the unity of form and matter? It is the *proximate* matter that Aristotle declares one with form. The proximate matter is the matter closest to the form in contrast with the ultimate matter, which is water, earth, and the elements. The matter closest to the form is the hand, the heart, and the other organs of an animal or comparable organs of a plant. The form, as we saw in H.2, is the actuality or, better, the function of the matter. As noted earlier, Aristotle claims that the hand severed from the body ceases to be a hand because it cannot function. It follows that the organs are matter just because they *are* functioning. But their functioning together is also the form. Hence, as Aristotle says, the form and the proximate matter are, in a way, the same. Again, the matter consists of the bodily organs, each of these is an organ only when it is able to function, and it is able to function only when it is connected with the other functioning organs. Since the form is the organs' being able to function together, the form *is* the organs in a way.

An animal does not cease to be an animal when it sleeps because it retains the capacity to function fully. It is this capacity to function, rather than the actual functioning that defines the animal. In *De Anima* (II.1) Aristotle calls the soul, which is the form of a plant or an animal, a "first actuality." He means that, although it is an actualization of matter, it remains a potentiality for a higher actuality, the "second actuality." Another first actuality is being a musician. Someone with musical talent (=potentiality) comes, through practice, to have musical ability (=first actuality) that she exercises in playing an instrument (=second actuality). She is called a "musician" in respect of her ability, not because she is actualizing it by playing. So, too, the form that makes a substance be what it is is a capacity for further actualization, a first actuality. It is in this sense that the definition of a sensible substance includes matter, as Aristotle had claimed in E.1. The form contains a kind of materiality because it is a potentiality, and to be potential is to be matter, as we will see.

"Actuality" has a special, technical sense that Aristotle elaborates in book Θ, but the reason that actuality is a cause of unity can be understood simply from the idea of actuality as function. Aristotle had claimed in Z.17 that the form is the cause of a substance's unity. H.6 elaborates this point by identifying form as actuality. The material parts are one just when they function together or, more precisely, when they have the capacity to function together. Having a capacity to function together is itself a kind of function; it is a first actuality. This is why glue or rope makes, respectively, pages and sticks into a something: what unifies the parts is also what allows them to function together. Although in these cases the cause of unity seems to be concrete, the material parts are unified just when they have the capacity to function together. But, then, artifacts are not properly substances, as we saw. In the generally recognized substances, plants and animals, there is no glue or rope. There is just the potentiality that is the matter and the function or actuality that is the form.

Importantly, to define something by its form is to define it by its function. Thus, a house is defined through its being able to provide shelter for a human being and his possessions. In general, to be something is to have the capacity for an act that is distinctive of that thing. This is a central Aristotelian doctrine, and it is a key conclusion of the complex analysis that constitutes Z–H. The reason that the agreed-upon substances of Z.2, that is, plants and animals, are substances is that their parts function together. They grow, they reproduce, they change location, and so forth. The capacity for one of these functions, the one that is most distinctive of the particular substance, is the form of the thing.

H.6 illustrates the unity of form and matter by, surprisingly, talking about a bronze ball. The function of the ball is to roll, and it does so because of its shape. The bronze is the ball's matter, and the spherical shape is its form because it gives the bronze the capacity to roll that is distinctive of a ball. However, matter and form cannot be separated. It is the bronze, so-shaped, that has the capacity to roll; it is the shape, existing in the bronze, that gives it the capacity to roll. Even in this simple artifact, the form and matter are one, in a way. But the bronze also has other functions, in respect of being bronze, functions that it would have even if it lost its shape. Artifacts lack the organic connection between matter and form that genuine substances have. In a plant or an animal the organs and the functioning of the organs are virtually the same. The organs are matter just when each has the capacity for its characteristic function, and the form is just the capacity of all the organs to function together.

To define a particular substance it is not enough to say that all the substance's parts function together: that is true of every substance and does not explain what the substance is. The definition of a substance's essential nature must obviously express a function that no other substance has, for otherwise the formula would not define that substance. Thus, Aristotle declares in the *Nicomachean Ethics* that the proper function of a human being lies in the practice of reason because no other plant or animal possesses reason (1097b33–1098a4). Reason is mysterious because it is not associated with a particular organ. In general, though, animals are defined by their characteristic modes of sensation and motion, and these do depend on particular organs. Aristotle suggests that the organ distinctive of an animal is its heart (1044b15–17), perhaps because the heart is the seat of sensation. An animal's other organs function to sustain its primary organ. In general, the functioning together of a substance's parts serves that organ that defines the substance. Insofar as the functions of the other organs can be distinguished from that of the primary organ, the substance is not one. So, in a way, *all* the organs function together in one act that differentiates the substance from other substances, but in another way the capacity for the distinctive function that is the form belongs properly to one organ in contrast with other organs whose functions usually, but not always, support the primary organ.

Characteristically, Aristotle identifies form as actuality in book H with little fanfare and barely a hint of its significance. It is suggested in H.1, introduced in H.2, and put to use in H.6. But H.6

has long been regarded as an addendum to the main thrust of the discussion. We have seen that it contains the culmination of one of the central discussions of the *Metaphysics*, what is it for a thing to be something? The answer, at least for a sensible thing, is that to be something is to have material constituents that are capable of functioning together. A thing is one insofar as its parts move all at once. Thus, the boards and bricks become a house when they are so arranged that they can provide shelter for a man and his possessions. To be is to be something and to be something is to have an essential function.

It should be evident that beings whose parts have an organic unity are able to function together most properly because the functioning of their parts comes from themselves. Artifacts consist of parts that function together, but only because they are used or set in motion by someone. Because their function does not stem from the matter itself, the matter retains its nature when it is in the artifact; and it constitutes, together with the artifact's form, an accidental composite. Accidents, too, amount to functions of the substratum to which they belong, but they cannot exist separately from the substratum.

Questions for reflection:

1 Is H.6's identification of the form and matter of a composite substance consistent with Z.7–9's argument that form and matter are not created in the generation of the composite? Does not Z.7–9 imply that form and matter must be distinct?

2 Is being some static state or, as Aristotle argues, a function and activity? In what sense could beings such as blue, four feet long, or stone be said to be functions? What must be true of thinking if it is to be the function that defines human nature?

Actuality: book Θ

Book Θ continues the discussion of the ways "being" is said by exploring potentiality (Θ.1–5) and actuality (Θ.6–9). A potentiality is "a starting point of change in another thing or in the thing itself *qua* other." In other words, something is potential because it can change if it is acted upon by something else, and the latter is also called potential insofar as it can change the first thing. Significantly, Aristotle characterizes different kinds of potentiality by the different sorts of agency. Thus, he distinguishes the rational agency of an ensouled being that can induce a change and also its opposite from the agency that brings about only one sort of change. A doctor, for example, can cause health but also knows how to make someone ill, in contrast with fire that can only heat. The same formula belongs to what is actual and to what is potentially that actuality.

What is possible, that is, what can be otherwise, is also said to be because it is potential. Something can be possible in respect of an attribute as yet unrealized, as possibly walking, or something can be possible if it does not exist but could exist. Aristotle hesitates to call the latter beings because they cannot be moved. They are potential, but not actual. In contrast, some things – such as, a square circle – are impossible and, therefore, not potential. Something is also potential if its existence is contingent on something else's existence and the second thing is possible. In this case, the possibility of the second thing will also depend on the possibility of the first, Aristotle argues. Still another respect in which something is called potential is if it is acquired through practice or study, such as fluteplaying and medicine. Such potentialities are acquired by an actual exercise of these arts.

It is interesting that something is potential in respect of an actuality it could attain and that its becoming actual depends on something else that is already actual. It is clear that potentiality is subordinate to what is actual.

Actuality, Aristotle explains, has been extended from motion with the thought that something in motion must be real, but an actuality also seems itself to be a motion (1047a32–b1). Most of what Aristotle identifies as actualities would ordinarily be called "motions," and the easiest way for us to think of an actuality is as special sort of motion.

In an important passage in Θ.6 Aristotle distinguishes actuality from motion. Before considering it, I note that motion is defined in the *Physics* as the actuality of a potentiality insofar as it is potential. (As we saw, in *Metaphysics* Θ every potentiality is defined in terms of the actuality, that is, the form, for which it is a potentiality.) The potentiality of bronze to be made into a statue exists in the bronze as a potentiality by virtue of its being bronze. This potentiality becomes actual in two different respects. First, it becomes actual when the bronze is being worked on by the sculptor, when the bronze is in the process of taking on the form that it will have as a statue. In this process, the bronze's potentiality becomes actual, but it does so *as potential*. Second, the bronze's potentiality becomes actual when the process is complete and the bronze has taken on the form that makes it a statue. At this point, the bronze's potential to become a statue is fully realized. The bronze's potentiality has become actual, but it has done so *as actual*. In other words, a motion is a process of acquiring (or losing) a form; and it is, thereby, an *actuality* of matter's potential; but the realization of this process that results in the statue is also an *actuality* of the matter's potential. In the former actuality, the matter continues to exist as potential; in the latter its potentiality is exhausted in the process of the form's coming to be in some matter.

It follows from this account that a thing in motion is always in the process of becoming something else. *Metaphysics* Θ.6 contrasts motion in this sense with actuality: whereas the thing in motion proceeds toward an end outside itself, an actuality – or, as it is sometimes translated, an action – contains its end within itself. Living, for example, is its own end; it is not done for the sake of something else. So, too, living well has no purpose beyond living well. Seeing is also its own end, even though it can also be for the sake of something else, such as thinking. Because an actuality has always attained its own end, it is outside of time, as it were. This is not to say that it need be eternal. It might cease to be, but it does not undergo a process of coming to be. It just is or is not.

Whereas the actuality is itself unchanging, it comes to be present with matter in the composite. This actuality is the form. As we saw in Z.7–9, the form remains unchanged in the generation of the composite. The composite is in motion, and the motion is the acquisition of a form, that is, an actuality; but the actuality remains unchanged.

A motion is, thus, ontologically distinct from an actuality. Motion and actuality are different kinds of entities. As I said, an actuality is best thought of as a peculiar kind of motion, a motion that never winds down or alters and that does not proceed toward an end distinct from itself. In contrast, what Aristotle terms "motion" is a process of actively being potential, and the potential is as such just when it is being realized, just when a matter is taking on a form. So the actuality is always just what it is; the motion is never what it is and is always becoming something else.

Even so, an actuality comes to be present through a motion, for the form that something in motion acquires is an actuality and the thing in motion is a potentiality specifically for that actuality. As Aristotle explains in Θ.7, it is not any matter that is potentially a man; not earth and water, but also not even the seed. The seed needs to be deposited in something and undergo a change. What is most properly termed "potentiality" is something that would become actual of its own accord if it were not interfered with. So a seed, properly disposed, is a potentiality when it is actualizing itself; that is, when it is in the process of acquiring the form. When the plant or animal is mature, it sustains itself. That is to say, the form of the animal is the function that is characteristic of it and that sustains the animal in existence. Again, the development of the seed into an animal is a coming to be, a motion; but the animal exists as an actuality, a functioning that sustains itself.

Θ.8 raises the question whether the potential or the actual is prior. For us, the question is usually posed as, which came first, the chicken or the egg? It is frequently mentioned as an example of an unanswerable question. Surprisingly, Aristotle argues that the chicken is prior. It is not that he has forgotten that every chicken was an egg before it was a chicken. He knows, too, that the egg came from another chicken which itself was an egg. So in one sense the process must continue indefinitely, and that is the sense that *we* focus on. But there is another way to look at the issue of temporal priority. We saw that a potentiality is always understood through the actuality for which it is a potential. Actuality is prior in definition. But it is also prior as an efficient cause because it is necessary for there to be an actually existing thing to act on something that is potential to realize that potentiality. The actual fire acts on the paper to bring it to flames; the carpenter with an idea of a table in his mind acts on the wood to produce the table. Even the seed that seems to develop by itself requires an actuality to produce it and then to deposit it in the proper place. The sequence might continue indefinitely in time, but the causal efficacy comes from the chicken, not the egg. Hence, the chicken needs to be prior.

Again, the egg will develop into a chicken, unless something else interferes. But the egg is the material; it is the pre-existing chicken that is the cause, and thereby prior in time to the egg. In respect of the other types of priority, it is even more obvious that the chicken is prior. As I said, it is prior in formula because the egg is understood through the formula of the essence of the chicken. The chicken is prior in substance because the egg and the entire process of development are so ordered and structured as to produce the chicken. That is to say, the egg develops in the way that it does because of the end of its process of development. It is the chicken that governs the path that the seed takes towards becoming a chicken.

All the potentialities Aristotle discusses in the first part of book Θ are connected with motion, and though motion is a kind of actuality, it is defined through the actuality that it attains or loses. The actuality that is the end of motion is a form. Since there are motions in many categorial genera (quality, quantity, and place), there must be forms in each of these genera that serve as ends of motion, and these forms are actualities. The actualities in the other categorial genera depend on the substances in which they inhere. And these substances, in turn, depend on their forms, forms that we know to be actualities. Hence, all the other actualities are led back to the actualities that are the forms of substances. Form, specifically, the form of a substance, is, evidently, primary in the actuality/potentiality schema of being, just as it is primary in the schema of the categories.

In Θ.9 Aristotle talks about mathematical proofs that depend on constructions. These constructions exist potentially in the initial diagram, but it requires a geometer to actualize the construction. Aristotle says that the cause of the construction is the intellect of the geometer, an actuality (1051a29–33). Hence, even in the categorial genus of quantity, actualities are prior. But these actualities and those in other categories always belong to some substances. Hence, the actualities, that is, the forms, of substances are prior to all else in this schema of being.

Questions for reflection:

1 Do you think Aristotle has successfully resolved the question of which came first, the chicken or the egg?

2 Can you think of examples from contemporary thought of potentials that are actualized without the action of pre-existing actualities of the type realized?

Truth: Θ.10

Aristotle had discussed truth in thoughts and statements in E.4, and set it aside because that sort of truth is not a being. Θ.10 considers the truth that is a being. If the idea of an objective truth seems alien, we have only to recall Augustine's claim that God is truth. Aristotle's notion of objective truth differs from Augustine's. His idea is that if the truth of thoughts and statements depends upon combinations and separations of things, then those things are causes of truth. As causes, they must somehow have what they cause. In particular, Aristotle is thinking of things that are always combined or always separate, like the diagonal of an isosceles right triangle and incommensurability with its sides and like a substance and its essential attribute. It is not just the *assertion* of their combination that is true; the *combination itself* is true, and the separation of these natures is false. The combination is a being, the separation a non-being.

What, though, about incomposites? Aristotle claims that truth is simply contact with them. Because they are simply one, their constituents cannot be separated nor, therefore, can they be false. Moreover, to grasp them is to know them; one cannot be mistaken about them. Importantly, an incomposite exists as an actuality. If it had potentiality, it would be a plurality of form (actuality) and matter (potentiality) and, thereby, not be incomposite.

The incomposites that are grasped simply must be the forms or essences of substances. Aristotle explained at length in book H how an essence of a substance is one. It is an actuality of a matter that is, we saw, one with that matter, in a way. This form is not the pure actuality we will encounter in book Λ. It is incomposite in a way, not absolutely incomposite. The composites that are true because their constituents are always united are composites of the substances and their essential natures. On the other hand, the things that are false because their constituents are never united are composites of substances and those attributes that *cannot* belong to them. Although Aristotle does not say so, we can see that these composites that are always true or always false depend upon substantial natures that are each incomposite.

The convergence of primary being

The most striking result to emerge from the discussion of the different ways of being is that the same being is primary in every way of being. That is to say, what is primary among categorial beings is primary among actualities/potentialities and also primary among true/false. It is clear that the same being is also presupposed by accidental beings. This being is the form or essence of substances. It is, Aristotle argues, an actuality and an incomposite.

Although Aristotle inquires into "what is substance?", he answers this question by finding the primary nature in respect of which things are called "substances." Thus, it is in respect of its form that a composite is a substance, that a universal like animal is a substance, and so forth. Since everything that is a substance is so by being related to this primary substance, and since every being is a being by being related to some sort of substance, all beings are related, directly or indirectly, to this primary substance. This is the nature of being that Γ referred to as "being *qua* being" without defining. It is now clear that the nature of any being is *its* own form/essence/actuality and that this latter is defined through the form/essence/actuality that, because it is one in number and formula, defines a substance. In other words, the answer to the question, "what is being?" is the form/essence/actuality that makes a substance be a substance.

At first glance, this answer might seem trivial, for Aristotle is, in effect, answering that what makes a being "what it is" is the being's "what it is to be" (the literal meaning of the Greek phrase generally translated as "essence"). This answer is reflexive, but not trivial for two reasons. The first is that Aristotle identifies essence as form and actuality. The form unifies the material parts; they are one just insofar as they have the capacity to function together. A thing is defined by its function; its nature is that function that is most characteristic of it, that function in the performance of which its parts move together. Thus, the form of a thing's matter is the capacity of that matter to function as a single entity. The second reason the answer is not trivial is that the nature of being is *some particular* being. It is often said that for Aristotle to be is to be something, but readers do not always realize why this is so. The nature of a being is an internal part of it, its own form. We saw in book Γ that the answer to the "is it?" question asked of being is that, indeed, being is; that is, that there is a quasi-genus of being insofar as each being has a nature. This nature is the substance of the being. It follows that each being *has* a substance and, more strongly, *is* its own substance. For it to be is to be what it is. Yet, when we inquire of being, "what is it?," we cannot find a single nature shared by all beings. Hence, Aristotle seeks the primary nature in respect of which things are called beings. Now no composite can be primary because the composite is a plurality and any plurality presupposes something that is one. Some things that we might have thought to be incomposite, like white and a length, can be seen to be composite because they always inhere in something else, a substance. Only what is independent or the principle of what is independent can be primary. A substance is an independent being. It is, thus, only of substances that the principle of the thing is primary. It is primary because it is what the substance is, its characteristic function.

This primary nature exists with matter. As such, it is not separate and independent, except in thought. Someone might want to dispute this claim on the ground that Aristotle identifies the nature with its proximate matter in H.6: if the composite is separate and the form is the composite, then the form is separate. However, Aristotle identifies form and proximate matter only "in a way," only insofar as each is the capacity of all the parts to function. (The organs [the matter] are each capacities to function and the form is the capacity of all the organs to function together.) In another way, form must remain distinct from matter, for the form comes to be present in the matter. Moreover, the same form is present in *many* distinct matters. How can the form be numerically one if it belongs to many distinct composites? Form is the cause of a composite's being one. How can that part of a substance responsible for making it a single substance belong to multiple substances? I do not think Aristotle can answer these questions, but he does not think that they undermine his conclusions. On the contrary, they support his conclusions. The form that Aristotle identifies in sensible substances has limited intelligibility. It does not exist by itself, nor can it be grasped by itself. Its intrinsic connection with matter is manifest in its being a first actuality and not a pure, complete actuality. It follows that the form of sensible substance is not the highest principle. The highest principle will be separate, not merely in thought, but absolutely separate. Finding it is the task of the third part of the *Metaphysics*.

The second set of *aporiai* in book B concern the unity of the principle of being. The central books of the *Metaphysics* identify this principle as form/essence/actuality. Insofar as it is form and essence, it is one in formula. Insofar as it is an actuality, it is numerically one. Form has the types of unity requisite to be a principle, but it has them only in a way. Again, there must be a higher principle.

One: book I

Book I is rarely read. Its subject, unity, seems to be peripheral to the main line of argument of the *Metaphysics*. However, it is crucial for understanding the central books and for inquiring into the highest causes, the inquiry that occupies the third part of this work.

First, book I is parallel to the central books. Just as the latter explore the nature of being, so the former explores the nature of one. Whereas the primary being in each of the ways "being" is said turns out to be the same, there is no convergence among the primary ones. This fact helps greatly to explain the central books. I.1 opens by describing four main ways "one" is said. A similar account appears in Δ.6, but I.1's account omits some of what appeared there, namely, generic and material substrata. These are ones that, Z had argued, are not properly substances. The ones that do appear in I.1 are substances. They fall into two groups: the ones defined by indivisibility in motion and the ones defined by indivisibility in thought. These groups are distinct because all ones defined by motion have matter, whereas the primary ones defined by thought do not.

It follows immediately that there is no single one that is primary in both groups or, consequently among all the ones. Hence, Aristotle claims that the "essence of one" is sometimes something that is one in a primary way and sometimes something "closer to a word." Explaining this claim, he compares the essence of one to the essence of element. The latter could refer to some element, such as earth or air, or to the formula of an element, that is, "to be a fundamental constituent." This formula expresses what it is to be an element, but it is not itself a thing nor is it the essential nature of any element. So, too, the formula of one is: (a) to be indivisible, or (b) to be the first measure of a genus, or (c) to be the measure of quantity. None of these is the formula of an essential nature. They are verbal formulae that, as we will see, characterize a color, a tone, and other entities whose essential natures are not defined as unities. What makes something one is not what makes it what it is.

It is, therefore, striking that the essence of being, that is, being *qua* being is *not* merely a verbal formula but a thing: essence is form and actuality. Consider a particular being like animal. The essence of an animal, that is, the "what it is to be for an animal," is, we saw, the form that unifies the material constituents by being their actuality. In general, the essence of being is essence, and essence is the thing. In contrast, the essence of one is a verbal formula that is not a thing. These claims are not word play: there is an intrinsic reflexivity in the nature of being that is not present in the nature of one. To be sure, being also has a unity, and, indeed, the unity of being is one. However, the unity of being is substance, and substance is one because it is an actuality, a being. In short, unity always depends on being.

We saw that the central books' inquiry into what being is becomes an inquiry into the primary being upon which all other beings depend. To inquire into what one is will be to examine the various things called "one" and the different formulae in respect of which they are so called. Again, the formula that defines something is the formula that signifies its being. The formula that signifies its unity does not define a thing. Rather, it belongs to the thing in respect of the thing's being. We could say that one or unity piggybacks on being. Indeed, it is only because there is a science of all beings that the various ones can also fall under a single science.

According to Aristotle's account in book A, Presocratic metaphysics centered around the problem of the one and the many. This problem is central to metaphysics because metaphysics itself is one science among many particular sciences. However, it is what Aristotle might have called "prior for us." The problem of being is "prior in nature," and it is through resolving it that the problem of the one and the many or, rather, *problems* of one and many are resolved. Problems of one and many remain important for the particular sciences. In tracing their resolution to the problem of being, Aristotle is laying grounds to understand how the particular sciences depend on metaphysics. Again, the essence of being is some thing, whereas the essence of one is either many things or one verbal formula.

I.2–9: what is one?

Having elaborated the essence of one, Aristotle seems to have answered the question that the eleventh *aporia* asks, "what is one?" However, he has not resolved the *aporia* because he has not undermined the assumption that generates it. Book B had mentioned two answers: the one is a substance and the one is a substratum. We know that the one cannot be a substance because one is a universal and no universal is primary substance (Z.13–16). Nor can the one be a substratum because there are *many* substrata; for example, the elements earth, air, fire, and water. Aristotle denies that *each* of these elements is one by itself; Z.16 claims each is one only insofar as something can be fashioned from it. It is only potentially one and, thus, not a first principle. The eleventh *aporia* arises from the assumption that one is a first principle. Aristotle recognizes that one is a mathematical principle. It is the principle of number, and number, in turn, is the principle of lines, plane figures, and solids. However, as we saw, a thing's nature is prior to its unity. It is in respect of its nature that a substance is indivisible in formula, for each substance has a formula that cannot be divided into a part that is the formula of the same thing or of something else (see Δ.6.1016a32–b6; Z.4.1030a28–b6). The essential nature that the thing's formula expresses is prior to this indivisibility. Again, being is prior to one.

Even so, there is a way in which a being is a principle because it is one. It is, first, a principle of a count. We can count the number of chairs because some chair serves as a measure in respect of which others of the same kind can be counted. This is a type of *quantitative* measure. More importantly and more surprisingly, each genus contains a being that serves as a *qualitative* measure of the genus. Aristotle's paradigm is the genus of color. White is the one of color because all other colors are composed of it and its privation, black. He is not talking about mixing white and black paint. Rather, as we learn later in book I, the differentiae of white and black are two contraries, compressing and dilating. The other colors are, as it were, between white and black in the sense that their differentiae are proportions of compressing and dilating. As something becomes whiter, it acquires a greater percentage in white's differentia. To say, then, that all other colors are composed of white is to say that its differentia helps to define them. They are all kinds of whiteness, in different degrees, in the sense just explained.

This intra-generic structure is important for the particular sciences, for they are each concerned with knowing some one genus. Our concern here in metaphysics is with understanding *that* there is a contrariety that marks off the species of a single genus as "other in species." There is, in color and other genera, a maximal otherness between different species in the same genus. On the other hand, there is also an otherness that falls outside a genus, "other in genus." Things that are other in genus are in distinct genera, and there are no intermediates between them. Categorial genera, like substance and quantity, are other in genus and so, as we will see, are the perishable and imperishable. They fall under no one genus.

The perishable and the imperishable: *I.10*

I.2–9 are often seen as a scattered collection of texts. However, the distinctions Aristotle makes in these chapters elucidate the notion of a species that is a qualitative measure of other species in the genus and prepare the way for the argument in I.10 that the perishable and imperishable do not fall in one genus. Aristotle explains three of the four types of opposites by locating them as constituents of the genus. (1) Possession and privation are the primary contrariety in a genus, and they serve as differentiae through which (2) contrary species are defined. The possession is the differentia of the species that serves as the one in the genus, the species through which other species are defined. These other

species are, accordingly, (3) relatives in respect of the one species
that is their measure. What distinguishes these other species from
the species that is one in the genus is their difference or, as we
usually call it, the differentia. That is to say, the contrarieties within
a genus serve to define its species.

Elucidating the structural components in the genus allows
Aristotle to argue that perishable and imperishable entities cannot
be instances of the same genus. This conclusion is important
because it means that perishable entities cannot be defined through
their indestructible paradigms, as Plato had tried to do. It also
partially answers the tenth *aporia* of book B, whether the principles
of destructible things are indestructible.

Aristotle's argument in I.10 is straightforward. A single thing
can be both black and white at different times because, insofar
as it is one of these, it has the potential to become the other.
Something is indestructible if it has no *capacity* to be destroyed.
If it were somehow to become destructible, it would have to have
had, all along, the capacity to be destroyed and, thus, to have
been destructible. Likewise, if something that is destructible were
to become indestructible, then one and the same thing would be
capable of being destroyed and not capable of being destroyed.
It follows that perishable and imperishable are not accidental
attributes, that is, attributes that might or might not belong to
a thing, but are essential attributes of whatever they belong to.
However, they are also contradictories, the fourth type of opposite.
Hence, there is nothing common to what is perishable and what
is imperishable: they are other in genus. It follows that a man,
for example, cannot belong to the same genus as an imperishable
man, the form of man. The sensible man cannot, then, be known
through or measured by the form of man, as Plato supposes.

This conclusion is significant because Aristotle himself needs
a separate principle. The central books show that form is the
primary substance because it is in respect of it that other things are
substances and beings. Form is an internal cause that is, in a way,
the same as the structured matter of an individual plant or animal
(H.6). However, the form also comes to be realized in an individual,
and thus requires an external cause. This external cause is another
form of the same sort that exists in another individual substance,
the parent. In order that this chain of causal events continue, there
must be some other cause that is itself eternal. This cause must

exist somehow *separate* from the substances being generated. We know from I.10 that the cause cannot be an eternal version of the same substance. We also know that this cause cannot be the one itself, because book I shows that a thing's oneness is subsidiary to its being. The rest of the *Metaphysics* is devoted to showing what the cause is and is not.

Book K: a reformulation of the problem

Book K appears to be another version of material from books B–E and the *Physics*. It is often cited as proof that the *Metaphysics* was not composed as a single work. Scholars have speculated that a student's lecture notes were somehow included along with Aristotle's text. Of course, we cannot prove that book K was part of the *Metaphysics*, but we can see that its content is necessary for the aim of metaphysics and that the book makes very good sense as it stands.

The reason book K has not been understood is that readers have not properly appreciated the earlier books of the *Metaphysics*. I suggest that book K reinterprets the issues and solutions of these earlier books in the light of what has emerged from them. We saw that the fundamental problems raised in book B are three: (a) how there can be one science of metaphysics, (b) how its principle is one, and (c) what its first principle is. Each of these problems breaks into multiple *aporiai*. The first two problems, (a) and (b), are resolved in books Γ–Θ. However, the principle they show to be one is the form of the composite substance. Since this principle comes to be present in matter, it requires another cause outside of itself. If this latter also comes to be present in matter, it requires still another cause. Ultimately, there must be a highest cause that is separate from matter. In other words, the principle that the central books show to be one is an internal principle of sensible substance that cannot be the first principle. The latter must be a substance that is separate and eternal. There is no way to arrive at this principle by continuing to consider the sensible substance; for the eternal, separate substance belongs to an entirely different genus. We need to make a new start and that requires reinterpreting what we have done.

In particular, book B's first set of *aporiai* assume that all beings must be included within metaphysics somehow, but there are various obstacles to a science that would treat them all. They are resolved by introducing an expanded notion of the genus that can *encompass* all beings. In contrast, Book K is concerned to delimit the boundaries of metaphysics so as to *separate* it from the particular sciences. Thus, although the first four *aporiai* look much like they did in book B, Aristotle poses the fifth *aporia* by noting that "the science we are seeking," that is, metaphysics, can deal neither with the causes mentioned in the *Physics* nor with the objects of mathematics; that is, neither with perceptible substances nor with those that cannot be perceived. He then adds another *aporia* to this group, whether the matter of the objects of mathematics falls under metaphysics or some other science (1059b14–21). Aristotle resolves these *aporiai* by explaining how metaphysics treats the subjects of the other sciences, even while differing from them. Whereas physics treats being insofar as it is moving and mathematics treats being insofar as it is quantity, metaphysics treats being insofar as it is being. Insofar as these other sciences also treat being, they are parts, or rather, species of metaphysics (K.4). However, Aristotle assumes here that each science treats a substratum and its attributes, and he speaks about "being insofar as it is being" ("being *qua* being") as a substratum, indeed, as the substratum of the accidental categories. We can see that to treat "being insofar as it is being" is to treat all the substances in the categorial genus of substance and all the other beings that are their attributes; whereas to treat "being insofar as it is moving" is to treat only some of these substances, sensible substances, and some of the other beings, namely, the attributes that they can acquire or lose. That is to say, book K tacitly assumes the results of the previous books when it explains how the first set of *aporiai* are resolved. It does not reject Γ's solutions; it reinterprets them by drawing on a more refined understanding of "being insofar as it is being." The essential nature of being has now turned out to be substance in the sense of a categorial genus, in contrast with the extremely broad sense of substance we saw in Γ, any essential nature. Likewise, although book K devotes two chapters (5–6) to arguing for the principle of non-contradiction, Aristotle is not concerned with whether the principle holds of all beings, as he was in Γ, but with whether a categorial substance has contrary attributes.

The second group of *aporiai* concern the unity of the principle. K.7 begins to answer them with what looks like a summary of E.1, the chapter that begins his earlier response. Both of these chapters distinguish metaphysics from physics and mathematics, and both speak of a nature that is separate and immobile and, thus, universal because it is primary. K.8 argues that there is no science of what is accidental, as did E.2–3. We would have expected Aristotle to continue book K with a discussion of the other ways of "being" that is comparable to E.4–Θ. Instead, he introduces a discussion of the principles of motion, a topic he had treated in the *Physics*. The principles of motion are form, matter, and the privation of form; and form is actuality. Whereas *Metaphysics* Z–Θ emphasize that the principles of sensible substances are one (in number and in species) and separate, at least in thought, K.9–12 shows these principles to be one, but *not* separate. The source of the difference is obvious: the central books explore the principle of substance insofar as it is a being, whereas K.9–12 elucidates the principles of *all* the categorial genera that admit change.

In the central books, what is most properly substance, the substantial form, is a self-subsistent principle of a static entity. Insofar as form and matter are one, this entity admits no change. But form and matter are one only "in a way." From another perspective, form and matter remain distinct, and sensible entities come to be when the two are united. There must be a first cause of this motion. What is the nature of this first cause and how does it cause motion? This is the subject of book Λ. Book K shows why it is necessary to ask that question, and we will see that it is of a piece with the opening chapters of Λ.

Question for reflection:

1 Aristotle resolves *aporiai* by finding a single doctrine that undermines arguments on both sides. Is this procedure itself undermined by book K's alternative account of the principles? In other words, does book K's alternative resolution of the second group of *aporiai* undercut the ground for accepting the first resolution in the central books?

Book Λ: Aristotle's first principles

Book Λ is often read as an independent treatise. However, its initial assertion of the primacy of substance can be readily understood in the context of book K's discussion of the principles of change in *all* genera. Whether all these genera together, that is, the universe, constitutes a whole or a "succession," substance is primary. If the universe is a whole, substance is the first part because everything else exists through a relation to it and nothing exists apart from it. If the universe is a succession, it would consist of substance succeeded by quality and then quantity. Substances are first because they are simple, and the other beings follow.

There are three sorts of substances: (1) those that are sensible and destructible, the subject of the central books, the last part of book K, and the first five chapters of Λ; (2) those that are sensible and indestructible, the heavenly spheres; and (3) those that are not sensible and not destructible.

Many readers have thought that Λ.1–5 repeat what we know from the central books and the *Physics*. However, these chapters make an essential contribution to the inquiry into first causes. The last lines of Λ.1 together with all of Λ.2 argue that the causes of change in all genera that admit of change are three: a thing's form or nature, its privation, and its matter. The last is a potentiality for a specific type of form. Λ.3 adds a fourth cause, the form that exists in another substance of the same kind or, in the case of attributes, in the mind of the craftsman. Aristotle is making an analogy between the principles of each genus. The four principles of change exist within each genus, but as different natures. Three of them belong to a single individual; the fourth belongs to another individual that somehow acts on the first individual.

The analogy Aristotle sketches in Λ.2–3 is the analogy he uses to define the one in book I. We saw there that within each genus there is a species that is the one in that genus because the other species of the genus are defined as some proportion of its differentia and the privation of this differentia. Change occurs when something comes to possess a greater or lesser proportion of the differentia. Thus, something that is black becomes whiter when it acquires a greater proportion of the differentia that defines white (cf. I.7). Aristotle claims that there is a one in the genus of substance as well, and he presumably means that there is a species of substance whose differentia serves as a principle in respect of which the differentiae of other substantial species are defined. One substance does not change into another, but any particular substance comes to be when its matter acquires the differentia that defines its species. Thus, the three principles of Λ.2–3 – form, privation, and matter – are the three principles of book I – the differentia of the species that is one, its privation, and the genus. The external cause is the form, or differentia, as it exists in another individual of the same species or in the mind of an agent.

Λ.4–5 raise an important question: are causes and principles the same for all beings? Universally and analogically, they are the same: form, matter, privation, and the external principle. On the other hand, there is no nature that is common to both the genus of substance and the genus of relation and, thus, no nature that could cause both. Any element would have to belong to some one categorial genus and, thus, could not be an element of entities in other categories. Nor can being or one be an element because they belong equally to the whole composite and its constituent parts. It follows that the causes of different things are different.

The cause that is universally and analogically the same is the one. The cause that differs in different genera is the being of each thing, that is, its essential nature. If the one were the first cause, the analogical structure of the universe would also be fundamental, and all things would have the same causes.

The one cannot, however, be primary. We saw earlier that unity belongs to something in respect of that thing's form, that is, in respect of its being. A thing's essential nature accounts for its being one, and not the other way round. Aristotle argues here that it is not the universal that causes change, but the individual form as it exists in a composite. The cause of you is not man universally, but your father because only the latter exists or existed as an actuality and only an actuality can act upon a matter and cause matter to realize its potential to acquire form. The universal father is not an actuality and, thus, has no causal efficacy. Except insofar as it is in the mind of a craftsman, the universal is not an efficient cause. On the other hand, insofar as attributes are caused by substances, the latter are the principles of all things. If, then, there is a first cause of substances, there will be a first cause of all beings. Λ.6–9 are devoted to showing that there is such a cause and what it is. The final chapter of Λ shows how this cause orders the universe.

Question for reflection:

1 Aristotle's analogy is based on the principles of motion, but there is not motion in all genera. Does this fact undermine the analogy?

The unmoved movers

In the *Physics* Aristotle says, famously, that the cause of man is man, but also the sun. He means that the oblique course of the sun is responsible for seasonal changes that are necessary for the plant and animal life that sustains man. The sun belongs to Aristotle's second class of substances, those that are eternal but sensible. He argues that the heavenly spheres that contain the sun and other heavenly bodies are eternal. This second class of substances is crucial for his argument for the existence of the third class of substances, the class that constitutes the first causes. Time is the measure of the motions of these spheres: a year is the circuit of the sun, a month the completed motion of the moon. Time cannot come to be or be destroyed because if it were, there would be a time before time existed and a time after it ceases, each of which is a contradiction. Moreover, since time is a measure of the motion of the spheres, if it came to be, there would have to be some other motion that brought about the motion of the spheres, and the measure of this prior motion would be time; this initiating motion, however, would be caused by a previous motion, and so forth. If there cannot be a first initiating motion, motion must have always existed. If motion has always existed, there is no reason to suppose that it will cease to exist. If it were going to stop, it would have done so already. Moreover, the motions of the heavens are circular: they need never end because they never reach an end point.

The existence of eternally moving heavenly bodies would seem to be at odds with Aristotle's account of motion. A motion is the actuality of a potential insofar as it is a potential (*Physics* III.1–2). When a thing's potential is realized, the motion ceases. Thus, the motion of housebuilding realizes the potential of the boards and bricks to be a house. When the potential is realized, the house exists and the motion comes to an end. There is no obvious end of a circular motion, but there is also no reason that it should continue indefinitely. Given the nature of motion to complete itself and cease, the existence of an eternal motion is problematic. It can only be explained by an eternally acting cause. A cause that acted at some times but not others would require some other cause to spur it to act. Nor can this cause contain any potentiality because, again, actualizing a potentiality requires an additional cause that is actual. A cause that moves something by contact is affected and altered by what it moves, but to be affected requires potentiality. It follows, then, that an eternal motion requires a cause that is without potentiality and that acts without being acted upon. Such a cause is purely actual. Insofar as it moves the spheres without being moved by them, it is an unmoved mover.

This argument shows that there must be such a cause, but it does not show what the nature of that cause is. The human mind grasps something by becoming the form of that thing. The form of the unmoved mover is an actuality without matter, but insofar as a human mind is the *potential* to grasp forms, it is not fully actual. It follows that the human mind cannot come to grasp the form of the unmoved mover without ceasing to be a human mind. We can, though, come to appreciate what this substance is like. It is, Aristotle claims, divine.

How does this substance move the heavenly spheres? Since it does not impart motion through contact, it must cause motion in another way. Aristotle proposes that the unmoved mover causes motion as the object of love. Just as the object of love spurs to action what loves it, so too the unmoved mover moves insofar as other substances strive to be like it. Thus, plants and animals reproduce in order to attain through their species something of the eternity of the unmoved mover. The heavenly spheres continue in circular motion in order to attain through motion something of the eternity of the immobile: always moving in the same way they imitate what always is in the same way. So, the highest cause is a final cause. It does not cause motion as an efficient cause would, by bringing what is at rest into motion. It causes motion insofar as what is already in motion imitates it. We cannot help wondering what started the motion, but this question is nonsensical if the universe is eternal. Motion always existed. The cause of motion accounts for the universe's order.

Since such a cause is proven to exist because of the eternal motion of a heavenly sphere, there will be as many causes as there are spheres. Just how many spheres there are is a matter for astronomy, and Aristotle is unsure which account is correct. According to one calculation, there are 47 distinct heavenly motions; according to another 55. There will be as many unmoved movers.

It is clear that the unmoved mover is thinkable in itself; for it is an actuality, a form without any matter; and matter cannot be thought. So, lacking matter, the unmoved mover should be most thinkable. The unmoved mover is a being of pure intelligibility, even if it cannot be comprehended fully by human thought, as we saw. Moreover, the unmoved mover is purely actual, and the actuality that exists without matter is thought. It seems plausible, then, that the unmoved mover is the intellect. This latter is not the human faculty of intellect, though our faculty does partake of it. Nor is the intellect a faculty of a higher being, say, God. Instead, Aristotle takes intellect to be a substance. The intellect thinks the object that is most thinkable and most worthy of being thought. Hence, the intellect thinks itself. In the *De Anima* Aristotle argues that we know a thing when its form comes to be in our minds or, better, when our minds come to be this form. In a sensible thing, form exists with matter; in our minds, it exists without matter. The intellect that Aristotle identifies as the unmoved mover also thinks an object without matter. The object most worthy of being thought is the object that lacks all matter, namely itself. Hence, the divine intellect that moves without itself being moved is thinking itself. As such, it is truly self-subsistent and, therefore, a substance.

As Aristotle argues in Λ.9, if the divine intellect thinks about something better than itself, it is not most divine. If it thinks of something less than itself, it makes itself worse. If it changes, it would have to have a potentiality, but it is purely actual. Hence, the divine intellect can think only of itself. Evidently, the first cause is a thinking about thinking. The subject thinking is the same as the object thought. Even this distinction between subject and object does not exist in divine intellect, for if it did, this intellect would be a composite and thought would change in passing from one part to another.

Aristotle does not explain which of the unmoved movers self-thinking intellect is. Medieval readers tended to identify the latter with the unmoved mover that moves the lowest heavenly sphere. Some more recent readers have supposed that a plurality of unmoved movers is inconsistent with Aristotle's account of self-thinking intellect. It seems more plausible to suppose that each unmoved mover is a self-thinking thought. Since we do not know the essence of any unmoved movers, we cannot say what it is that each one thinks. We can surmise that each unmoved mover is different from the fact that different spheres have different circular motions. Thus, Aristotle seems to endorse a plurality of unmoved movers, each of which thinks itself.

We might wonder whether some unmoved movers think other unmoved movers, as well as themselves. This would be a plausible way to account for the ordered structure of the cosmos. The first unmoved mover would think itself only, the second would think itself and the first, and so on. However, this would mean that all but the first unmoved movers would be thinking a plurality and that would seem to imply motion. However, there is a *first* unmoved mover, the mover of the outermost sphere, and this sphere moves the spheres beneath it. So each of the other spheres is moved both by its own unmoved mover and by the higher spheres.

In this way, the unmoved movers order the heavens, and the heavens, in turn, order the sublunar world. The final chapter of book Λ claims that the good of the cosmos lies in both its order and its cause, just as the good of an army lies in its leader and in the organization he brings about. At first glance, the analogy seems weak because the general is an efficient cause and the unmoved movers final causes. However, Aristotle probably has in mind an idea he expresses in the first chapter of the *Nicomachean Ethics*, that the general sets the ultimate end, victory, towards which the ends of the various subordinate arts (such as horsemanship and bridle-making) contribute. So, too, the unmoved movers set the end towards which the other substances contribute. That ultimate end appears to be eternity. Each substance contributes to this end in its own way by being what it is. As Aristotle explains, the higher the substance, the less it is able to deviate from the ultimate end. Just as the freeman is less able than the slave to set aside the ends of the household, so the eternal substances do not deviate from their ends. We know from elsewhere that destructible substances contribute to the end of the cosmos by reproduction: the species, rather than the individual, is eternal.

This end-oriented order contrasts strongly with the beginning-oriented orders that are the implicit consequences of accounts that generate the cosmos from elements. All these latter accounts have one contrary act upon another, but that is impossible, Aristotle claims, for the contrary does not itself change, but something else changes, namely, the matter that the contraries act upon. It is not the form of the bad that can become good, but some thing that is bad can become good. It seems that other philosophers spoke of one thing's acting on its contrary because they were trying to *generate all things*. In order to generate all things, they needed to generate matter. In contrast, Aristotle assumes that matter must pre-exist any generation. He is, thus, unable to generate all things.

Moreover, if the good is an efficient cause, as other philosophers suppose, it is puzzling what it could gain by generating or moving matter, for it is already the good. The good cannot account for the existence of material beings. If, alternatively, the principle is a number, as some philosophers suppose, how can it generate a line? Further, numbers that are principles will generate an "episodic" cosmos, one in which one stage is followed by another just as number is the principle of lines, and lines the principles of planes. Such a cosmos would lack unity and, thereby, lack the good that Aristotle shows to exist in the cosmos. For these reasons Aristotle rejects the claim that the good is the efficient cause of the cosmos.

Questions for reflection:

1   Aristotle argues that there are first principles of the cosmos, but what exactly do these principles explain, and what are they not able to explain?

2   Insofar as the highest causes cannot explain everything, there is room for particular sciences of individual genera of being, sciences such as physics and mathematics. Do these particular sciences along with the highest science account for everything or is there still something unexplained?

Book M: mathematicals and forms

Books M and N are seldom read. They argue against implausible philosophical positions whose original expositions are not extant, positions that have no modern proponents. Moreover, since

Aristotle sets out his own first causes in book Λ, the subsequent books are anti-climactic. Or so it has seemed. We will see that these books are essential contributions to his metaphysical project. In particular, they not only refute the claims that mathematicals and forms are the first principles, but also show how these entities depend upon Aristotle's own first principles. The arguments are too complicated to pursue thoroughly here, but a brief sketch of these books helps to understand the project of the whole. Book M examines mathematicals and forms, two entities that Plato and his followers in the Academy thought to be substances. Aristotle raises three topics of inquiry in M.1: (1) whether and how mathematical objects exist; (2) the forms; (3) whether forms and numbers are the substances and principles of beings. Just where each topic is covered is not always clear. The last lines of M.1 together with M.2–3 address the first topic. M.4–5 clearly contribute to the second topic. M.6–10 argue against the forms being numbers, though I suggest that these chapters contribute to all three topics. First, they expound numbers, thereby adding an account of the objects of arithmetic to M.2–3's account of the objects of geometry. Second, they explore the forms, specifically, the form numbers. Third, M.6–10 show why forms are not principles of beings and, in M.10, how forms exist. The rest of the third inquiry, whether numbers are the substances and principles of beings, is addressed in book N.

Mathematicals

Do mathematicals exist separately? There is good reason to suppose that they do, for Aristotle argues first that to suppose them not to exist separately leads to contradictions. First, two or more actual entities would exist in the same thing; namely, the thing and the geometric solid that forms its boundary, both of which are solids. But two solid entities cannot exist in the same place at the same time. Furthermore, each thing would be indivisible because whereas every solid is divided at a line and every line divided at a point, each point is indivisible. Since any division of a thing would be a division at some point, and the point cannot be divided, the thing cannot be divided.

On the other hand, there are good reasons to think that mathematicals do exist in sensible substances. If they were separate, not only would there be another solid besides the sensible thing, but since that solid is itself delimited by planes, there would also be planes besides the sensible planes. For the same reason that there is another solid besides the sensible solid, there would be another separate plane besides the sensible plane. Which of these two separate planes would mathematics treat? Since planes are delimited by lines, and lines by points, the same reasoning shows the existence of multiple separate lines and points as well. Not only would there be a multiplicity of separate mathematical entities, but there would be no way to decide which of them is the subject of mathematics. Furthermore, if mathematical entities did exist apart, there would be a cosmos that exists separately from the sensible cosmos, as well as animals besides sensible animals, an absurdity. Another objection to separate mathematicals derives from the thought that since mathematicals delimit sensibles, the latter are constructed from them. Even if sensible entities could somehow be constructed from lines and points, the sensible solids would be prior in being because what is posterior in generation is prior in being. Finally, even if mathematicals are included in the defini-tions of sensibles substances and are, thereby, prior in definition to them, they are not prior in being; for consider the definition of pale man as a composite. It includes the definition of pale along with the definition of man, but pale is still posterior in being because it cannot exist except in man or some other substance. Even if a substance were defined by its shape, the mathematical shape could not exist except as the delimitation of this or some other substance. Hence the shape is posterior in being to the man. On the other hand, if the shape were separate, it would be prior in being to the substance it delimits. Hence, it cannot be separate.

In short, M.2 draws out an *aporia*: mathematical entities cannot exist in sensibles, but they cannot exist separate from sensibles either. Like other *aporiai*, this one is resolved by rejecting or modifying the assumption that generates it. Although Aristotle does not say so, the critical assumption here is that mathematical entities exist only as actualities. It is only if they are actual existing substances, that mathematical solids occupying the same place as sensible solids is a contradiction. On the other side, it is only if mathematicals are actual substances, that a separate mathematical cosmos would occupy its own place and that a mathematical plane would be prior in being to the sensible substance it defines.

We can appreciate that the assumption that mathematicals exist as actualities is critical in generating the *aporia* from Aristotle's account of mathematicals in M.3. He notes that it is possible to speak of motion apart from the nature of the thing that moves, and this amounts to treating motion *as* separate even if it does not exist separately. Similarly, the mathematician treats solids, lines, and so forth *as* if they existed separately even if they do not. Aristotle says that the mathematician treats a sensible insofar *as* it is a solid or a plane; to use the Latin translation, the mathematician treats the sensible *qua* solid or *qua* plane. Some scholars have spoken of this *"qua"* locution as a means of filtering out those predicates that do not belong to the sensible insofar as it is a solid or plane and treating just those properties that the sensible has in respect of either character. However, this understanding does not explain how M.2's *aporia* is resolved. Aristotle suggests the resolution when he claims that the geometers speak correctly when they speak of their subjects as beings because a being can be in actuality ("fulfillment") or "as matter" (1078a21–31). If geometric objects existed as actualities, he would not need to say this. His point must be that geometric objects are beings even though they exist "as matter," that is, potentially. As Aristotle notes here, the geometer treats solids and other geometric objects as if they were separate, even though they are not. If solids existed separately, they would have to be actualities. Hence, Aristotle means that the geometer treats his subject as an actuality even though it exists as a potential being. The potential solid exists in the sensible thing "as matter."

If mathematical entities do exist in sensibles potentially, both sides of M.2's *aporia* vanish. The arguments for separation are arguments against mathematicals being in sensibles. The first objected that two solids would occupy the same place if mathematicals were in sensibles, but this is not problematic if one solid is actual and the other exists potentially. The second claimed that sensibles would be indivisible because points are indivisible, but there is no objection to dividing a sensible solid at a point if the point exists potentially in the solid and comes to exist after a division is made. On the other hand, the absurd consequences of separating mathematicals that support the other side of the *aporia* do not arise if geometric objects are *not* separate but exist in sensibles as potential beings.

The notion that mathematicals exist potentially also appears in the *Physics*. Aristotle argues against the idea that a line is composed of points. It is rather that the point comes to be by dividing the line. Before the division, the point exists in the line potentially. The line itself results from the division of the plane, which latter is the division of a mathematical solid. In short, all geometric entities exist potentially in a sensible substance. M.3 explains that even though geometric objects are potential beings, mathematicians treat them as actualities. The mathematician, through his intellect, actualizes the mathematical entities.

Insofar as they are potentialities, mathematical entities cannot be first principles. Clearly, they depend upon the principles upon which sensible substances depend.

Questions for reflection:

1 Aristotle is speaking mainly about geometric objects. What difficulty does he need to address to treat number analogously as existing materially? Can he give an adequate account?

2 Modern mathematicians deal with entities much more complex than lines and solids. Can Aristotle's account of mathematicals be applied to them?

3 Aristotle's arguments suggest that *multiple* mathematical entities exist potentially in the same sensible. Does this consequence undermine his solution to the *aporia*?

M.4–5: forms

The next section consists of arguments against Platonic forms. These or similar arguments appear in A.9. Famously, Aristotle claims here that Socrates was convinced by Heraclitus's contention that all sensible things are changing and, hence, seeking to define the virtues, he posited them to be unchanging forms so that they could be objects of knowledge. Although Socrates did not separate these forms of virtues, those who followed him, that is, Plato and the Academy, did separate them. Aristotle claims that Socrates sought to arrive at universal definitions inductively from examples.

Does Aristotle mean to say that Socrates' forms were like his own, immanent in sensibles but unchanging? No, for he thinks

Socrates' forms are universals, but he argues that his own forms are not universal (Z.13–16). That the Socratic form, as well as the Platonic form, is universal is problematic because each is also an individual. Aristotle avoids this difficulty for his own forms by means of extended senses of these notions. His form is one in formula and, thereby, knowable; hence, it is universal in an extended sense. Likewise, his form is one in number, insofar as it is an actuality, and thereby individual, though also in an extended sense.

Aristotle presents Socrates as seeking universals that exist *in* sensibles in order to have knowledge of individual virtues. In contrast, Plato and the Academy posited the forms as universal but *separate*. Aristotle goes on to argue that none of the arguments for separate forms is successful and that the forms do not contribute anything to accounting for sensibles. They do not allow us to know sensibles and, since they are not efficient causes, they cannot cause motions in sensibles.

Evidently, whether forms are universals that are in sensibles or universals that are separate from sensibles, they are not causes through which sensibles can be known. There seems to be an implicit *aporia* here that parallels the *aporia* we saw in M.2–3.

Form numbers: M.6–9

Plato's followers and, perhaps, Plato himself made the forms numbers. We get a glimpse of why Aristotle thought they did so in an argument he sketches in B.6. There are multiple sensible pairs; hence there must be some character in respect of which each is a pair. This character is the number 2. Each sensible pair is an instance of this number. However, there are also multiple instances of the number 2. They are necessary for computations like 2 + 2. Since wherever there is a multiplicity with the same character, there must be some unity in respect of which the multiplicity is the same; thus, there must be some form in respect of which each number 2 is 2. Since the multiplicity of number 2's are all of the same kind, a form that is only one in formula will not be different from them. Rather, the form must be both one in formula and one in number. This form is the two itself. This latter seems to be a form number of the sort that Aristotle considers in M.6–10. The units in number 2's can be added together, but the units in the 2 itself cannot, nor can they be added to anything else.

This last distinction is probably what Aristotle refers to when in M.6 he distinguishes between numbers whose units are comparable and numbers whose units are not comparable. There is a 2 and a 3 with, respectively, two units and three units that can be added together to produce another number with five units. In this 2 and 3, all the units are comparable. There is another 2 and 3, namely, the two itself and the three itself, whose respective units are not comparable and which, thus, cannot be added together. Nonetheless, the units within the two itself may be comparable with each other or they may not be comparable with each other. In the latter case, no unit of any form number would presumably be comparable with another unit of any form number. To this range of possibilities, Aristotle adds that although Plato endorses both forms and mathematicals, some in the Academy reject mathematicals and endorse only form numbers, while others reject forms and endorse only numbers.

None of these accounts is plausible. The numbers with comparable units are just collections of units. They have no unity and, thus, cannot be proper forms. On the other hand, those numbers with non-comparable units are still defined by the number of their units. If the units within a number are not comparable, they cannot be counted, nor could they define the number. If they are comparable with each other, but not with units from other numbers, the Platonists are saddled with the problem of differentiating the one sort of unit from the other – an impossibility inasmuch as the units are simple. To summarize too quickly a lengthy discussion, Aristotle shows in detail why there is no way that there could be form numbers. Thus, this version of the forms doctrine must also be rejected.

Universals: M.10

After extensive arguments against there being forms, it seems surprising for Aristotle to inquire in M.9 whether forms could be causes of sensibles. The question acknowledges that, despite all the arguments, forms do exist. Aristotle's task is to determine what those forms are, that is, to find a legitimate place for Platonic forms in his own metaphysics. This he does in M.10.

This chapter begins by asking whether substances are separate or not. If (1) they are not separate, they could not be principles that require no further principles. If, though, (2) they are separate, then it seems to be impossible that they have principles, for these principles can be neither individual nor universal. To support this last claim, Aristotle presents a version of the last *aporia* of book B: (A) principles that are individual are elements, and if these are the only principles, there could be nothing besides the elements. Moreover, these principles could not be known because knowledge is of the universal. On the other hand, (B) if the principles were universal, either (a) substance would be a universal or (b) something that is not a substance would be prior to substance. Since substance is not a universal (as argued in Z.13–16), the universal would have to be prior to substance. But, we have seen that all other beings depend on substance.

We saw one solution to this last *aporia* in Z–H. There the form is both one in formula and one in number and, thereby, universal and individual in extended senses of these latter terms. However, the form discussed in Z–H is a substance that is *not* separate. Thus, it falls under option (1) here, and it cannot be a first principle. The substance that is separate is the individual composite, and the issue here is how it can be known if knowledge is of the universal and the universal is not its principle. Since the universal does not exist within the individual, to grasp the latter through the universal, even as an instance of the universal, is to fail to grasp it as it is.

In a claim that recalls his account of mathematicals in M.3, Aristotle says in M.10 that there are two senses of knowledge: one actual, the other potential. To know a universal is to have the latter; to recognize an instance of this universal is to have the former. Thus, someone who grasps color universally has the ability to recognize a color, and someone who grasps some particular color universally, say blue, has the ability to recognize blue. Someone who perceives a color he identifies as blue is actualizing these abilities. When he sees something blue and recognizes it as a color, he has actualized this potential and grasped an actual object. Evidently, the individual object can be known either universally, as something that has a color, or actually as this object with this color. To know through a universal alone is to know potentially. Apparently, to grasp the individual actually requires grasping the actuality that is its form.

In the *De Anima* (III. 4) Aristotle claims that we know something when its form comes to be in our minds. This is an actual and immediate grasp of an actual individual. In effect, M.10 adds that to know what *kind* of a thing it is we drop down a notch, as it were, and grasp it as potentially determinate, that is, as a universal. Since like knows like, my being able to grasp an individual by having a universal in my mind entails that the universal must also exist somehow *within* the individual I grasp. Just as it exists in mind as a potentiality, it must exist as a potentiality in the individual object that I grasp. It exists as the material of the form, the genus, as we saw in Z.12, or as the matter of the actuality that is the form of the individual.

If this interpretation of the chapter is correct, M.10 is an account of how universals exist in sensibles. They are present in matter as potentialities. The Platonic forms are universals as are the form numbers, and Aristotle has argued against their existence as principles of things. Nonetheless, there are universals that are principles of knowledge, and Aristotle still needs to account for them. Like mathematicals, the universal exists in an individual substance as a potential. In the existing individual object, this potential is actualized as the thing's existence. The individual exists because its form is an actuality. Nonetheless, the individual contains within itself the potentiality for this actuality, the universal species or genus, that allows it to be grasped through a more general thought. We saw that mathematicals exist in substances potentially but are actualized by thought. So, too, the universal exists in substances potentially. In this case, though, a certain sort of thought preserves the potentiality of the universal. When the universal is actualized in an immediate grasp of an object, the potential is realized in an actuality. Analogously, the guitarist's knowledge of music is potential until he plays his instrument.

How universals exist is a problem that has puzzled many philosophers. The universal is a single character that is common to many. It is usually said that it cannot be in any of the many because it belongs to all and that it cannot exist separately if it is an essential character that an individual must have. Aristotle's solution is that the universal exists in each individual as a potentiality. This latter is not the *actual* character that exists in the individual but the capacity for it. So the universal cannot be identified with any of the many that fall under it, but it is potentially all of them.

Aristotle has actual knowledge in mind when, in Θ.10, he speaks of direct noetic contact with the simple and distinguishes it from demonstrative knowledge. The latter is universal and, therefore, a potential knowledge. It is legitimate and important, but it depends on actual knowledge. According to medieval Scholastic philosophers the universal is just the form as it is grasped by the mind, whereas the individual is the form as it exists in nature. However, we have seen that M.10 distinguishes the universal as the potential way of knowing an object that can also be known actually. To know in the latter way is to grasp its form. Again, the object can be known universally because the universal exists within it. Socrates can be grasped universally as a man or actually as the man that he is. The latter differs from the former only insofar as the form is in act.

Question for reflection:

1 Many philosophers, some influenced by Aristotle, have tried to understand what a universal is, and their answers are often divided into nominalism, conceptualism, and realism, according to whether they think a universal is a name, a thought in a mind, or a real being. Does Aristotle's account fit under any of these rubrics? Compare his solution to the problem of the universal with solutions advanced by other philosophers.

Book N: mathematicals as principles

Book N completes the discussion of the third question raised at the beginning of book M, whether forms or mathematicals are principles of things. We have seen that forms or, rather, universals are principles of knowledge, but subordinate to Aristotle's own forms. There is good reason to think that mathematicals are indeed principles of things, but we also know from M.2–3 that Aristotle thinks they are subordinate to substances and, thus, *not* principles or, at least, not first principles. We may well wonder why Aristotle is raising the issue again. Indeed, many readers think book N has little that is new to contribute to metaphysics. This view is incorrect. Although Aristotle has refuted the notion that mathematicals are first principles, they are certainly principles of some sort. Recall Aristotle's claim in book I that there is a one in each genus. We saw that this one is a species and that other species in the genus are composed of it and, sometimes, the species that is its privation. Aristotle thinks that there are determinate *proportions* between the differentia of the species that is one and the differentia of the species that is its privation that define the differentiae of the intermediate species of the genus. It is not accidental that he identifies five colors between black and white and the same number of species of other sensible kinds. The same mathematical proportions are at work in each of these genera. The sciences that know these genera need to grasp the mathematical principles at work in the definitions of their species. So, even though mathematicals are not first principles, they are principles. The issue in book N is how mathematicals can be principles of physical beings, and it is an issue just because we know that the *first* principle of any genus is the essential nature of the genus. Since mathematicals belong to another genus, the genus of quantity, it is hard to see how mathematicals can play any role in a science that treats a genus of substance or quality. Also at issue in book N is what the principles of mathematicals are.

N.1 begins by arguing that although all things are from contraries, the contraries exist in some underlying subject. This subject or, rather, the substratum is necessary because one contrary cannot act on another contrary, as the Academy supposes. Contraries are defined through the possession and privation of a form. Their definitions do not change. If the bad becomes good, it is *something* bad that has changed, not the bad. Insofar as the contraries depend upon a substratum in which they inhere, they cannot be first principles.

Plato's followers in the Academy conceive of the one itself acting on its contrary, but they disagree on whether this contrary is plurality, the unequal, the indefinite dyad, the other, or something else. Besides the omission of the subject in which the contraries exist, the Academy is also mistaken in supposing that a single line of generation will produce all things. As Aristotle reminds us in N.1, the one is a measure that presupposes some underlying substratum, such as, tones or colors. There are, thus, different ones for different genera. If the one differs in each genus, then so does its contrary: there is no single contrary to the one because there is no single one.

Even those in the Academy who identify the contrary of the one as the indefinite dyad speak of many dyads and generate different entities from them. From the more and the less they derive numbers; from the long and the short come the line; from the broad and the narrow come the plane; from the deep and the shallow come solids (N.2.1089b9–15).

At the beginning of N.2, Aristotle argues against eternal entities, such as numbers, either being generated or consisting of parts. If they come to be, they would also be able to pass away – in which case they are not eternal. Likewise, an eternal being with parts would have the potential not to exist because the parts are potentially separated. What has the potential not to exist is perishable and, therefore, not eternal. Although the Academy thinks numbers are eternal, it inconsistently claims numbers are generated and contain parts.

Not only are numbers not generated themselves but they cannot play a role in the generation of other things. Numbers do not cause things to move. Nor can numbers be the good because they are not the ends of motion. Number cannot be formal causes either. The boundaries of substances are not numbers but lines or planes. Even if a substance were defined by a ratio, the numbers would merely be the matter of the ratio and indicate the relative amounts of one element to another, for example, three parts fire and two parts earth (5.1092b16–23). Thus, it is the elements that are the true matter of the substance. A number of some element presupposes a nature of that element, and the natures of a substance's elements are responsible for the substance more than their numbers. (Greek thinkers do not recognize a proportion or a fraction as a number.) In short, numbers are not causes as any of the four kinds of cause.

What, then, are numbers? Aristotle's answer is easy to miss. The one in each genus is some species or instance of that genus. It follows that there is number in each genus. Insofar as its nature is some number of ones, each other species is a number or, at least, is defined by numbers. Also, the number of instances of a genus is defined in relation to a single instance that serves as the one of that genus. In short, just as the one differs in each genus, number differs in each genus. Number in color is not the same as number in tones. It follows that there is no number that stretches across genera. That is to say, the numbers are defined through a genus, rather than the genus's being defined through numbers. The last chapter of book N speaks of the seven vowels, the seven notes of a scale, the seven stars in the Pleiades, and the seven against Thebes as a mere analogy. The causes of each are rooted in its genus. Seven is not the same number in each genus.

Nonetheless, seven is a principle within each genus. There is a reason that there are seven notes, but it must be found within the genus and it is not the same reason that there are seven vowels. The mistake of the Platonists is to try to constitute sensible things from numbers. Aristotle, in contrast, extracts numbers from sensible things. He mentions one method of extraction in N.1 in the context of criticizing the Academy's generation of number from one and its contrary. It is the method that most readily comes to mind. Think of a group of objects, such as the people in a room. Any one person can serve as the measure of a count of people. However, the number of people in a room is relative to the unit. It follows that this number is a relation. The latter is one of Aristotle's categorial genera of being. Aristotle thinks that numbers as well as relations are attributes, and each attribute must belong to some *single* substance. In this case the attribute is being in a group of such-and-such number of people in the room. This attribute belongs to each person in the room. It is a relation, but it is also a very superficial attribute because it is altered by someone else's leaving or entering the room. In other words, an attribute of one person can be altered by something else's changing, even if he remains entirely unchanged. One of Aristotle's objections to Plato's account of number is that it makes relations that are posterior be principles. In short, the number that is a count of distinct objects is not the number that is a principle.

Aristotle has another way of extracting numbers from sensibles, a way that is consonant with their being principles of sensibles. We saw in M.3 that geometric entities exist potentially in sensible substances. They are actualized by our mind's disregarding a substance's other characters and considering only its nature as a solid. This solid can be divided, mentally, to produce other, more regular solids. Their surfaces can be considered alone, as can the lines that bound those surfaces, and as can the points that limit the lines and into which the lines can be divided. We need only take one more step to see the numbers that also exist in the sensible substance potentially. The points that limit the line or into which the line is divided can be counted, as can the parts of the line. This number belongs to the substance. Like the geometric objects we saw earlier, this number exists potentially in the substance but is actualized by the intellect of the mathematician. This number is a principle if it belongs intrinsically to the substance's nature, such as, the two that is the number of a human being's feet or the ten that is the number of fingers. Alternatively, since there is some species that measures the other species in a genus, the other species are defined as some number of the differentia of the species that is one or through a proportion between this differentia and the differentia of the species that is its privation in the genus. The point is that there are numbers that are *defined* through the essential natures of species of the genus. These are numbers that are principles through which the genus is known and also exist potentially within individuals in the genus.

There is a certain affinity between this account and the Academy's accounts. The genus and, especially, the line are dyads. There is a more and a less in both: the long and the short in the line (1088b9–15), more and less of the contrary species that delimit motion in a genus (I.7.1053b23–27). The one that is imposed on these continua, possibly multiple times, marks off multiple portions, in something of the way that the Academy imagines the one itself to act on the dyad. The genus and the line are indeterminate matter that becomes determinate species and lengths through an act of thought. The crucial difference is that Aristotle denies that there is a single one that acts and a single dyad that is acted upon. The one differs in each genus, there is no generation from the one, and the one depends upon the genus. Substance is prior to number. Number does not cause substance; substance causes number.

It follows that any science can look for numerical relationships within the subject matter it studies. Since the numbers are determinations of that subject, they will help us to know it. The numbers pertinent to different subjects may seem the same, but the numbers at work in the sciences of music and grammar are not numbers from the genus of quantity, but numbers proper to their subjects. That the same numbers are at work in different genera stems not from the nature of numbers but from the nature of the subjects. To suppose otherwise, to think that it is the numbers that count, leaves us open to including the seven of the Pleiades and the seven enemies of Thebes within a single science. In short, there is a legitimate role for mathematics in particular sciences, but that fact does not make these sciences branches of mathematics. Importantly, the presence of mathematics in the particular sciences does not undermine Aristotle's claim that to be is to be in act, for the mathematicals are themselves actualities insofar as they exist by our mind's actualizing a real potential in an indeterminate subject.

Philosophers traditionally look to the highest science, metaphysics, to provide a foundation for the particular sciences. Aristotle holds that the particular sciences each treat either a sensible substance or accidents of substances, such as quantities. Mathematics treats quantities, but it treats them as if they were separate, that is, as if they were substances. In mathematics the quantities are causes, but they depend on still prior causes that do not belong to mathematics, namely, the sensible substances in which they inhere. Since sensible substances, themselves the subjects of other particular sciences, are in turn dependent on supersensible substances, all beings can be traced back to these latter first causes. It follows that metaphysics, the science devoted to the first causes, knows all beings by knowing their first causes. Yet, we know little about these first causes other than that they are pure actualities, and they tell us little about the subject matter of any particular science. We have seen that the objects of mathematics are actualities of some sort. We have also seen that genera that constitute the subject matters of particular sciences are potentialities for the actualities that the sciences seek to know. That the objects of the particular sciences are actualities is of fundamental importance for those sciences. This is the sense in which metaphysics lays the foundation for these sciences: it shows that their objects must be actualities. Not only are metaphysics' own first causes pure actualities, but the *Metaphysics* also argues that to be is to be an actuality of some sort, that is, to have a defining function. It is the function of a thing or, most often, the *capacity* for a certain function that defines a thing as what it is. In sensibles, this function is possessed by some matter, but the function must be distinct from the matter that undertakes it. If the matter loses this capacity to function, the thing ceases to be what it is. A spade is a spade as long as it can be used to dig; it is no longer a spade when it cannot be used to dig. Since each particular science aims to grasp the essential nature of its subject genus, and since this nature is some sort of actuality, the particular science seeks an actuality. Since it is metaphysics that shows this essential nature to be an actuality, metaphysics lays the foundations of the particular sciences. Since, moreover, the pure actualities known by metaphysics are the ends of sensible substances, and since all other sensible beings depend on sensible substances, the pure actualities are the ends of all beings and, in this way too, lay a foundation for the particular sciences.

As important as the dependence of other beings on the unmoved movers is, it tells us nothing about the particular function that a triangle or any other nature has. To explore the particular function that constitutes the nature of the subject genus as well as the functions that define the one in this genus and the other entities is the work of particular science. This work can be carried out without reference to the first causes or to the striking parallels between the subject genus and all the other genera. That there is a one in each genus, that other species are constituted from its differentia, that the same proportions define these other species, and, accordingly, that the same numbers figure prominently in grasping multiple genera are all tokens of the existence of the same ultimate cause and the similarity of each genus to the others. This much is, thus, a matter of metaphysics. However, the particular actuality that defines the genus and the attributes that belong to the genus in respect of it are independent of the first principles and must, thus, be discovered by particular science.

We can understand this relation between metaphysics and the particular sciences in terms of still another distinction. First philosophy is the science of being, Aristotle declares at the opening of book Γ. Being is shown to be actuality in the central books. There are, though, many kinds of actualities, and the actuality that defines one entity differs greatly from the actuality that defines another nature. The final portion of the *Metaphysics* shows that all beings depend on the pure actualities that move without being moved. It also shows that one and number depend on the particular actualities within a genus. In short, metaphysics shows the priority of being to unity. The particular sciences presuppose some generic nature, and they seek its essence and actuality (E.1); but they aim to elucidate its various species and the relations of those species. While they recognize the priority of being to unity, the particular sciences explore the one along with number and proportions insofar as they belong to its subject. Thus, with the appropriate qualifications, we can say that whereas metaphysics is the science of being as being, the particular sciences each explore the one and the many that are defined through some particular being.

Questions for reflection:

1 Aristotle's justification for using mathematics in the particular sciences implies that there are different kinds of numbers in different genera. Is this a coherent doctrine of number? Is it too high a price to pay?

2 Why does the use of mathematics in the sciences need to be justified? Can you think of another way to justify this use?

Summary

A brief summary of a work as complex as the *Metaphysics* can hardly do it justice, but it is, nonetheless, important for appreciating it. Aristotle understands metaphysics to be the science of the first principles and highest causes of all beings. What are these principles and causes?

There are two highest causes and one first principle that is not a cause. Every cause is a thing of some sort. Most principles are also causes and, thereby, things or natures. However, the principle of non-contradiction is not a thing. It is the highest principle of knowledge because unless it holds, there can be no knowledge. Anything that can be rightly asserted and rightly denied in the same way at the same time cannot be known: it is no more one nature than it is not that nature. On the other hand, there can be no doubt that there is knowledge: doctors have special training that enables them to restore sick people to health far more successfully than non-doctors. The issue is which beings can be known. It is particularly important because Plato argues that sensible beings are not knowable. In contrast, Aristotle argues that the principle extends universally to all beings. Since the principle holds of what has a nature, it follows that every being has its own essential nature. This nature is not the nature of being, which latter is common to all, for even non-beings share this nature. Hence, a thing's having the nature of being will not insure that the thing cannot both be and not be at once. The nature it must have is the particular nature that makes it what it is in contrast with other beings. To be is to be something, and being is not a character over and above the particular nature that makes a thing what it is.

The first highest cause is the form of sensible substances. Aristotle argues that form is primary because everything else in a substance exists and is known through it. In the course of the central books, Aristotle peels away everything that might make a substance many. What remains is the cause of a composite substance's being one thing. This is the form, for the form unifies the material elements.

By "material elements," Aristotle means not the earth, air, fire, and water, that is, the elements that are primary, but the organs of an animal or plants, that is, what he calls "proximate matter." The form unifies these elements because they are one insofar as they have the capacity to move together, and this capacity for motion or function, is the activity or actuality that makes them what they are. Again, the material elements are one because they are able to move or function together. The form is just the capacity of the elements to function together. Since both matter and form are the material's capacity to function together, form and matter are one. However, they are only one only "in a way." The form and matter cannot be entirely one because the composite is not eternal. Rather, it is generated when form comes to be in the matter and destroyed when form ceases to be in this matter. Insofar as it and its matter are one, the form of a substance is the highest cause. On the other hand, insofar as this composite comes to be, there must be some other cause.

The route to this other highest cause is through motion rather than unity. One motion is caused by the motion of something else, and the latter motion, in turn, is caused by still another. But this sequence cannot continue indefinitely. There must be some first cause. This first cause is not a temporal beginning. Every causal sequence terminates in a first cause, but not necessarily in the same first cause or at the same time. Moreover, every temporal beginning we can imagine would be preceded by a time when it did not exist, a time before time. The apparent contradiction here forces us to reject the assumption that there is a temporal beginning. Rather, time is eternal. Since time is a measure of motion, motion must be eternal. From the eternity of motion, Aristotle infers the existence of *something* that is in eternal motion. This is a heavenly sphere. Motion in a circle has no natural stopping point, but it could not sustain itself forever because all motion not constantly renewed must eventually cease. To sustain a sphere in eternal motion, Aristotle posits an eternally acting causal agency, an unmoved mover that is pure actuality and moves by being an object of love. This latter is truly the highest cause. It is the first substance. It is not only a source of motion, but also the principle that allows there to be particular sciences, for physics is the science of being in motion and mathematics deals with entities that exist in sensibles materially, that is, potentially. Both sciences require that matter and form not be identical, unlike the actualities explored in the central books.

The two highest causes are, thus, not directly connected. The universe is not one. There is, however, a harmony of its parts that Aristotle may have in mind in Λ.10. Each substance strives to be like the unmoved mover, but it does not do so by imitating the unmoved mover's form but by seeking to imitate, to the extent possible, its eternity. Thus, Aristotle takes the propagation of the species to be caused by the unmoved mover and also the pursuit of knowledge mentioned in the *Metaphysics'* first sentence. Each individual strives for the unmoved mover by seeking to be itself, either by continuing itself in another of the same species or by grasping through the intellect the eternal principles. Fortuitously, it seems, in being oneself, each being performs the very functions that sustain the cosmos as it is. In this way, the destructible entities in the cosmos display a degree of continuity and harmony with the eternal principles that are their first causes.

CHAPTER FOUR

Reception and influence

No philosophical work has been more influential for philosophy than Aristotle's *Metaphysics*. One sign of its significance is that even though Plato is often its chief target, later Platonists, the so-called "Neoplatonists" devote a great deal of attention to it. Plotinus, for example, often reframes Platonism in Aristotelian terms. Thus, he ascribes actuality to Plato's principles in order to explain their connection with that of which they are principles, that is, that which emanates from them; and he identifies Plato's *nous* (mind) with Aristotle's idea that the unmoved mover is thought thinking itself. Whereas Aristotle argues that this latter is one, Plotinus sees it as a duality, namely, as the subject that is thinking and the object that is thought. Since he himself holds that a duality, that is, a two, cannot exist without some one, Plotinus posits a still higher unity, the one itself.

Contemporary readers are often surprised to discover that Plotinus thinks that Plato and Aristotle advance substantially the same philosophy. Of course, there is a certain fundamental similarity insofar as both Plato and Aristotle advance form as a principle, in contrast with other Greek philosophers who advanced material principles. However, Aristotle argues at length that there cannot be separate forms, as Plato thought. How can Plotinus endorse Plato's form without being subject to Aristotle's critique?

He may think that his own position is not subject to these arguments because his own forms do not exist as *separate* individuals. Each exists together with all the other forms in the realm of *nous*. Unlike *nous*, Plotinus's highest principle, the one, contains no parts. It is so thoroughly unlike anything sensible that Aristotle's claim that Plato's form was just an eternal version of a sensible could not apply to it, nor could it apply to a realm of *nous* in which each form implied all the others. In any case, some of Plotinus's innovations are responses to the *Metaphysics*' challenges to Platonism.

A Christian Neoplatonist like Augustine cannot abide separating the highest principle from the intellect. Hence, he moves the forms into God's mind. How the highest principle can be one then becomes mysterious. Indeed, it must be one even while it is three, Augustine claims. Thus, although Augustine has little to say about Aristotle, he seems to have taken to heart Aristotle's criticism of separate forms, or Plotinus's response to it; for, again, his forms do not exist as separate individuals.

The main thrust of the later medieval appropriation of Aristotle begins from an entirely different direction. For Aristotle, as we have seen, to be is to be something, that is, to be some form. It follows that a form just is a being. However, medieval thinkers take being as existence. It then becomes possible and, indeed, necessary to inquire into the causes of a form's being, a question that makes no sense for Aristotle. For Aristotle the form of a sensible substance can be present in a matter or, indeed, in many matters. In general, such a form comes to be present in a matter and can cease to be present with matter. Hence, the composite is perishable, even though its form is eternal. Although it belongs to the nature of such a form to exist in composites, the existence of any individual at any time is accidental. This existence cannot be deduced from the nature of the form. Nor can Aristotle's unmoved mover, a thought that thinks itself alone, know whether a composite exists. Hence, whereas the form just is, the composite may be or not be.

Medieval thinkers, however, were convinced that the first unmoved mover that Aristotle so eloquently proves to exist must be God. Subsequent unmoved movers could be angels, but God must know not only the forms, as Augustine had claimed, but the individual instances of the forms, for it is the latter that receive or fail to receive providence and salvation. For either of these, God must know whether or not an individual is. In this usage, "is" must mean "exists." Moreover, the God who created the world must be the cause of its existence and, ultimately, the cause of the existence of the individuals in it. With this reflection, the question becomes, what does "existence" signify? What does it add to form? Thus, medieval philosophers transformed Aristotle's concern with being into a concern with existence without even changing his terminology.

In other words, medieval philosophers developed Aristotle's notion of being into a concept that characterizes an individual composite so that the latter could be known. To illustrate, that a form comes to be in matter is a character of the form in general. That this particular form has come to be in some matter, that is, that it now exists, is an additional bit of knowledge over and above the form. This is a knowledge of an individual.

The question of existence is so powerful that the reader who recognizes that Aristotle does not see being as distinct from form can hardly help feeling that there is a hole in his philosophy in his failure to treat the existence of composite individuals. It is important to see that Aristotle does have an account of existence. As I said, he argues that the forms, that is, the essences, of sensible substances exist somehow within those sensible substances. It belongs to each such essence that it be in many individuals. The essence of human being, for example, persists because there are many human beings. Yet, any single individual is accidental. That this individual comes to be and the general way it comes to be are consequences of its essence, but no particular individual can be known. The medieval introduction of existence shifts the focus from the essence to the individual. For Aristotle it is the essence that is known either potentially as a universal or actually as an individual, but individuals as such are unknowable. Most medieval thinkers see unknowable individuals as a limitation of God's knowledge.

The medieval question is: what does the individual need, in addition to its essence, to exist and, thereby, to be known? One very important answer was given by the Persian philosopher, Avicenna (980–1037): existence is a simple character that is added to an essence. The cause of this addition is another being that already has existence. Unless it exists from itself, this other being must have acquired existence from still another cause, and so on. Since there cannot be an infinite sequence of causes, there must be one essence that necessarily exists. This essence includes existence.

Since this essence is the first cause and since nothing that is many can be a first cause, this essence must be one: it must *be* existence. This necessary being is obviously God. Avicenna identifies it with the first of the unmoved movers; the other unmoved movers are angels. Since everything else that exists derives its existence from this first cause, and since everything that happens does so necessarily because it is caused by this cause, Avicenna sees a suitably modified Aristotelian metaphysics as a rationally justified account of the principles of the Islamic faith.

Another important Muslim philosopher, Averroes (1126–1198), widely known for his commentaries on Aristotle's works, seems to hold a view that is closer to Aristotle's, namely, that being belongs to form. Some forms exist apart from all matter by virtue of their nature, and other forms, those of sensibles, come to be present in matter, but the multiplicity of their instances is accidental. Although he rejects creation, Averroes maintains that the existence of the world depends upon God and that the proof for this claim lies in the suitability of the world for the existence of man and the other substances that inhabit it (see *Faith and Reason in Islam*). In other words, the various types of sensible entities are sustained in their existence by the order and harmony of the whole world, and the latter, in turn, is sustained by a divine cause. In this way, existence belongs to each form by virtue of the connections of its instances with instances of other forms. It follows that Averroes regards existence as something over and above the form itself, at least, in the case of sensible forms. Moreover, the existence of these latter depends upon a cause, and if this cause is not to depend upon another cause, and the latter on still another, and so on indefinitely, then there must be a first cause that exists from its own nature, that is, a necessary existent. Although this last conclusion recalls Avicenna, Averroes thinks that material individuals are accidental and, thereby, without causes and unknowable. Hence, Averroes treats existence, but does not account for individual existence.

The obvious Aristotelian way to account for individual existence is to ascribe it to matter. An individual horse comes to be when its form or essence comes to be in matter. The essence comes to be present in matter when existing substantial essences reproduce themselves, and they do so with the aim of participating in eternity by resembling the unmoved mover. Although the latter is a cause of existence, the more immediate cause of any essence's existence is its own matter. For the essences of sensibles, to exist is to be enmattered.

"Matter" for Aristotle and the medieval tradition that followed him is not the determinate stuff we think about when we use this term. Aristotle uses "matter" to refer to what is potentially something else. Thus, wood is the matter for a table, whereas water or wool is not. Matter may have its own form, but it is always understood *as matter* in respect to the form for which it is the potential. It follows that matter is subordinate to the form and indeterminate in itself. We can now understand how paradoxical it would be to claim that the presence of matter adds existence to an essence. Matter takes its character from the essence it receives and is, thereby, secondary; if matter also conferred existence on form, it would thereby be prior to it. In respect of existence, matter would have an importance that is contrary to the priority of essence and form for which Aristotle argues.

On the other hand, the notion that existence is something simple that is somehow added to essence, as Avicenna claims, has its own problems. Since (I) an immaterial essence must be simple (cf. N.2), if it acquired existence, it would become a plurality and, thereby, something with the potential not to be. As such, it could not be the pure actuality Aristotle claims it is. It is more plausible to suppose that (II) an essence that exists in matter would acquire existence. Indeed, such an essence acquires existence just when it comes to be in matter. We saw that this essence is the cause of the unity of the material parts of the composite (Z.17). If, though, existence is something added to the essence, how is it related to the unified composite? If it does not belong to the composite, the *existing* composite would not be unified and the addition of existence would undermine the unity the composite needs to exist. If it does belong to the composite, then either (a) it, and not form, is responsible for the composite's unity or (b) form unifies not only material parts but also these parts and existence. Alternative (a) is contrary to Aristotle's analysis, whereas (b) allows the form to control existence, but it was because form is *not* responsible for existence that the latter was posited as something added to it. In short, the addition of existence to the form that unifies a composite does not seem compatible with the function of this form. Further, although an essence that acquires existence is presumed to exist as an individual, it is puzzling what could make this existing essence many and distinguish its instances from each other. Matter is usually said to do both, but Avicenna thinks matter has its own form, an indeterminate dimensionality. The only plausible source of individuality is the causal sequence through which the Necessary Existent confers existence on an essence so that it can exist with matter. However, this sequence is necessary and what results is necessary. Hence, the individual created and known by the first cause is devoid of free will.

Thomas Aquinas (1225–1274) draws on Aristotle's distinction between actuality and potentiality to advance an enduring solution to the problem of existence. Aristotle argues that matter is a potentiality for form or essence and that the latter is its actuality. Aquinas contends that form is, nonetheless, a potentiality for the actual existence of the substance. That is to say, he adds, as it were, another level on top of the Aristotelian hierarchy. The form may be the actuality of matter, but it is a potentiality for a higher actuality. The essence that exists in an existing thing also exists in my mind when I grasp the thing. The form in the horse and the form in my mind are the same, Aristotle claims. However the form of the horse that is in my mind cannot gallop or neigh. The latter belongs to the actuality that is the horse. For the essence to exist it needs to be able to function. This existing essence is an actuality that is realized concretely in the individual horse. To be is, then, to have the actuality for which the essence is a mere potential.

On this account an essence is actualized by its coming to be in a matter, but the actuality is not the matter. It is a realization of the form in act. Hence, Aquinas avoids making matter the cause of existence. Since existence is a further actualization of an essence, he also avoids making existence a simple addition to essence, as Avicenna had. Aquinas's interpretation of Aristotle and his account of existence were further elaborated and refined by subsequent Scholastic philosophers.

In short, Aristotle's idea that the existence of an individual instance of an essence is accidental along with his claim that there is no knowledge of accidents challenge the medieval notion that the highest cause, God, must know everything that follows from it. Avicenna addresses the issue by making existence something added to essence. Averroes makes existence an effect of the form, and Thomas Aquinas argues that existence is a further actualization of form. All three begin their own metaphysics from Aristotle's. It is not for nothing that medieval thinkers call Aristotle "the philosopher." His philosophy, especially the *Metaphysics*, was the beginning and the departure point for late medieval developments in metaphysics.

* * *

The continued importance of Aristotle's metaphysics can be seen in the fact that the founders of modern philosophy in the seventeenth century felt obliged to refute Aristotle. Thus, Galileo imagines debates between a modern physicist and an Aristotelian. Descartes begins his own metaphysics, the *Meditations*, by dismissing the evidence of the senses, a move that recalls Aristotle's insistence in A.1 that knowledge arises from sensation. Descartes goes on to sketch the relation of metaphysics to the particular sciences as one of root to branch, thereby graphically rejecting Aristotle's notion that metaphysics is the culmination of knowledge. Descartes argues that metaphysical reflection is a prerequisite for evaluating the claims of the senses. The God he argues for is a guarantor of the truth of our indubitable perceptions, that is, of our clear and distinct ideas, rather than the ultimate source and end of all motion, as Aristotle and Aquinas suppose.

The new paradigm introduced by modern philosophy is bodies in motions that are altered by outside forces acting upon them. Although individual substances seem to drop out of account, modern philosophers reintroduce substance, not as the self-subsistent individual but as an inclusive whole. Thus, Descartes seems to see three substances, God, matter, and soul. Spinoza reduces these to a single substance with two attributes, and Leibniz adds that there are an infinite number of such substances, all co-ordinated with each other and each containing within itself all the laws of nature. That is to say, continental rationalists of the seventeenth and eighteenth centuries did not reject Aristotle's notion of substance so much as reapply it. Instead of ordinary individuals, they identified larger, more encompassing substances that could contain within themselves multiple interacting bodies and the laws governing those interactions.

Their empiricist counterparts adopted a more skeptical view of the existence of substances. Thus, Locke argues that the subject of attributes is intrinsically unknowable, and Hume draws the same conclusion about the human mind. Berkeley sees clearly that science is not about individual substances or even substantial natures so much as streams of phenomenal properties.

In short, the central project of modern philosophers was the refutation of the Aristotelian/Scholastic notion of substance. They either introduced different entities as substances or they did without substance altogether. Modern science, that is, seventeenth-century Newtonian physics, is based on the interactions within a field of bodies that differ from each other in quantitatively measurable attributes, but not in their substance.

It is noteworthy that initial attempts to grasp the physics of bodies through forces on bodies proved inadequate. Scientists quickly introduced the notion of energy. The energy of motion, kinetic energy, is given by mass times velocity squared. However, when the body rests in its new position, energy is preserved as potential energy. The term "energy" derives from Aristotle's term for actuality, *energeia*. Hence, the Aristotelian distinction between actuality (or activity) and potentiality reappears as a central distinction in modern science. Nonetheless, the notion of substance plays no role in contemporary physics.

This notion has, however, made something of a comeback in contemporary metaphysics. Many contemporary philosophers have continued to see the cosmos as composed of individual subjects and their properties. However, contemporary philosophers have not endorsed Aristotle's notion of a thoroughly self-subsistent individual as the first cause. They have retained the scientific notion that laws describe the relations of attributes even while they take the individual entities governed by those laws to be something like Aristotelian substances. In short, Aristotle's metaphysical distinctions have continued to be influential in manifold ways even if his philosophy as a whole is no longer current.

GUIDE TO FURTHER READING

1 The *Metaphysics* in translation

Apostle, Hippocrates George, trans. *Aristotle*'s Metaphysics. Grinnell,
   Iowa: Peripatetic Press, 1979.
Barnes, Jonathan, ed. *The Complete Works of Aristotle*. 2 vols. Princeton:
   Princeton University Press, 1984.
Furth, Montgomery, trans. *Aristotle. Metaphysics. Zeta, Eta, Theta, Iota*.
   Indianapolis, Ind.: Hackett Pub. Co., 1985.
Hope, Richard, trans. *Aristotle. Metaphysics*. Ann Arbor: University of
   Michigan Press, 1960.
Lawson-Tancred, Hugh, trans. *Aristotle. Metaphysics*. London, England:
   Penguin Books, 1998.
Ross, W. D., trans. *The Works of Aristotle*. Vol. 8. *Metaphysica*. 2nd ed.
   Oxford: Clarendon Press, 1972.
Sachs, Joe, trans. *Aristotle's* Metaphysics. Santa Fe: Green Lion Press,
   1999.
Tredennick, Hugh, trans. *Aristotle. The Metaphysics*. The Loeb Classical
   Library. Cambridge, Mass.: Harvard University Press, 1956.
Warrington, John, trans. *Aristotle. Metaphysics*. Everyman's Library.
   London: Dent Dutton, 1966.

2 General commentaries on Aristotle

Ackrill, J. L. *Aristotle the Philosopher*. New York: Oxford University
   Press, 1981.
Barnes, Jonathan. *Aristotle*. Past Masters. Oxford: Oxford University
   Press, 1982.

—ed. *The Cambridge Companion to Aristotle*. Cambridge: Cambridge University Press, 1995.

Evans, J. D. G. *Aristotle*. Philosophers in Context. Brighton: Harvester Press, 1987.

Jaeger, Werner Wilhelm. *Aristotle: Fundamentals of the History of His Development*. 2nd ed. Translated by Richard Robinson. Oxford: Oxford University Press, 1967.

Lear, Jonathan. *Aristotle: The Desire to Understand*. Cambridge: Cambridge University Press, 1988.

Robinson, Timothy A. *Aristotle in Outline*. Indianapolis: Hackett, 1995.

Ross, W. D. *Aristotle*. London: Methuen, 1966.

3 Ancient and medieval commentaries on the *Metaphysics*

Alexander of Aphrodisias. *On Aristotle's* Metaphysics *2 & 3*. Translated by W. E. Dooley, and Arthur Madigan. Ithaca, N.Y.: Cornell University Press, 1989.

—*On Aristotle's* Metaphysics *4*. Translated by Arthur Madigan. Ithaca, N.Y.: Cornell University Press, 1993.

—*On Aristotle's* Metaphysics *5*. Translated by W. E. Dooley. Ithaca, N.Y.: Cornell University Press, 1993.

Aquinas, Thomas. *Commentary on the* Metaphysics *of Aristotle*. Translated by John Patrick Rowan. Chicago: H. Regnery Co., 1961.

Averroës. *Ibn Rushd's* Metaphysics: *A Translation with Introduction of Ibn Rushd's* Commentary on Aristotle's Metaphysics, *Book Lām*. Translated by C. F. Genequand. Islamic Philosophy and Theology. Leiden: E. J. Brill, 1986.

Suárez, Francisco. *A Commentary on Aristotle's* Metaphysics: *A Most Ample Index to* The Metaphysics *of Aristotle*. Translated with an introduction and notes by John P. Doyle. Mediaeval Philosophical Texts in Translation. Milwaukee, Wis.: Marquette University Press, 2004.

Syrianus. *On Aristotle's* Metaphysics *13–14*. Translated by John Dillon and Dominic O'Meara. Ithaca, N.Y.: Cornell University Press, 2006.

4 Contemporary commentaries on the *Metaphysics*

Annas, Julia. *Aristotle*'s Metaphysics: *Books M and N*. Clarendon Aristotle Series. Oxford: Clarendon Press, 1976.

Barnes, Jonathan, Malcolm Schofield, and Richard Sorabji, (eds) *Articles on Aristotle*: 3. *Metaphysics*. New York: St. Martin's Press, 1978.

Bell, Ian Hamilton. *Metaphysics as an Aristotelian Science*. International Aristotle Studies. Sankt Augustin: Academia Verlag, 2004.

Bostock, David. *Aristotle. Metaphysics: Books Z and H*. Clarendon Aristotle Series. Oxford: Clarendon Press, 2003.

Brentano, Franz Clemens. *On the Several Senses of Being in Aristotle*. Translated by Rolf George. Berkeley: University of California Press, 1975.

Broadie, Sarah. *Aristotle and Beyond: Essays on Metaphysics and Ethics*. Cambridge: Cambridge University Press, 2007.

Burnyeat, Myles. *A Map of Metaphysics Zeta*. Pittsburgh: Mathesis Publications, 2001,

Cherniss, Harold F. *The Riddle of the Early Academy*. New York: Russell & Russell, 1962.

Frede, Michael and David Charles, (eds) *Aristotle*'s Metaphysics *Lambda: Symposium Aristotelicum*. Oxford: Clarendon Press, 2000.

Gill, Mary Louise. *Aristotle on Substance the Paradox of Unity*. Princeton, N.J.: Princeton University Press, 1989.

Graeser, Andreas. *Mathematics and Metaphysics in Aristotle*. Bern: Paul Haupt, 1987.

Halper, Edward C. *One and Many in Aristotle*'s Metaphysics: *Books A-Δ*. Las Vegas: Parmenides Press, 2009.

—*One and Many in Aristotle*'s Metaphysics: *The Central Books*. 2nd ed. Las Vegas: Parmenides Press, 2005.

—*One and Many in Aristotle*'s Metaphysics: *Books I-N*. Las Vegas: Parmenides Press, 2013.

Irwin, Terence. *Aristotle's First Principles*. Oxford: Clarendon Press, 1988.

Katayama, Errol G. *Aristotle on Artifacts: A Metaphysical Puzzle*. SUNY Series in Ancient Greek Philosophy. Albany: State University of New York Press, 1999.

Kirwan, Christopher. *Aristotle's Metaphysics: Books Γ, Δ, and E*. Clarendon Aristotle Series. Oxford: Clarendon Press, 1971.

Krämer, Hans Joachim. *Plato and the Foundations of Metaphysics*. Albany: State University of New York Press, 1990.

Loux, Michael J. *Primary Ousia: An Essay on Aristotle*'s Metaphysics Z *and H*. Ithaca: Cornell University Press, 1991.

Madigan, Arthur. *Aristotle*. Metaphysics: *Books B and K 1–2*. Clarendon Aristotle Series. Oxford: Clarendon Press, 1999.

Moravcsik, J. M. E. *Aristotle: A Collection of Critical Essays*. Modern Studies in Philosophy. Notre Dame London: University of Notre Dame Press, 1968.

Owens, Joseph. *Aristotle's Gradations of Being in* Metaphysics *E–Z*. Edited with a preface by Lloyd P. Gerson. South Bend, Ind.: St. Augustine's Press, 2007.

—*The Doctrine of Being in the Aristotelian 'Metaphysics': A Study in the Greek Background of Mediaeval Thought*. Toronto: Pontifical Institute of Mediaeval Studies, 1978.

Politis, Vasilis. *Aristotle and the* Metaphysics. London: Routledge, 2004.

Reale, Giovanni. *The Concept of First Philosophy and the Unity of the Metaphysics of Aristotle*. Translated by John R. Catan. Albany: State University of New York Press, 1980.

Reeve, C. D. C. *Substantial Knowledge: Aristotle's Metaphysics*. Indianapolis, Ind.: Hackett Pub., 2000.

Shields, Christopher. *Order in Multiplicity: Homonymy in the Philosophy of Aristotle*. Oxford Aristotle Studies. Oxford: Clarendon Press, 1999.

Sorabji, Richard. *Necessity, Cause, and Blame: Perspectives on Aristotle's Theory*. Ithaca, N.Y.: Cornell University Press, 1979.

Witt, Charlotte. *Substance and Essence in Aristotle: An Interpretation of* Metaphysics *VII-IX*. Ithaca, N.Y.: Cornell University Press, 1989.

Yu, Jiyuan. *The Structure of Being in Aristotle's* Metaphysics. Dordrecht: Kluwer, 2003.

5 Selected articles

Albritton, Rogers. "Forms of Particular Substances in Aristotle's *Metaphysics*." *Journal of Philosophy* 54 (1957): 699–708.

Halper, Edward C. "Aristotle's Paradigmatism: *Metaphysics* I and the Difference It Makes." *Proceedings of the Boston Area Colloquium in Ancient Philosophy* 22 (2007): 69–103.

Klein, Jacob. "The Aristotelian Critique and the Possibility of a Theoretical Logistic." In *Greek Mathematical Thought and the Origin of Algebra*. Translated by Eva Brann. Cambridge, Mass.: MIT Press, 1968.

Kosman, L. A. "Substance, Being, and *Energeia*," *Oxford Studies in Ancient Philosophy* 2 (1984): 121–49.

Lang, Helen S. "The Structure and Subject of *Metaphysics Λ*." *Phronesis: A Journal of Ancient Philosophy* 38 (1993): 257–80.

Lear, Jonathan. "Aristotle's Philosophy of Mathematics." *Philosophical Review* 91 (1982): 162–91.

Nussbaum, Martha Craven. "Saving Aristotle's Appearances." In *Language and Logos: Studies in Ancient Greek Philosophy Presented to G. E. L. Owen,* edited by Malcolm Schofield and Martha Craven Nussbaum, 267–93. Cambridge: Cambridge University Press, 1982.

Owen, G. E. L. "Logic and Metaphysics in Some Earlier Works of Aristotle." In *Aristotle and Plato in the Mid-Fourth Century: Papers of the Symposium Aristotelicum Held at Oxford in August, 1957,* vol. 11, edited by Ingemar Düring and G. E. L. Owen. Studia Graeca et Latina Gothoburgensia, 163–90. Göteborg: Elanders Boktryckeri, 1960.

Rorty, Richard. "Genus as Matter: A Reading of *Metaphysics* Z-H." In *Exegesis and Argument: Studies in Greek Philosophy Presented to Gregory Vlastos,* edited by E. N. Lee, A. P. D. Mourelatos, and R. M. Rorty, 393–420. Assen: Van Gorcum, 1973.

6 Platonic background

Fine, Gail. *Plato on Knowledge and Forms: Selected Essays.* Oxford: Clarendon Press, 2003.

Miller, Mitchell H. *Plato's Parmenides: The Conversion of the Soul.* Princeton: Princeton University Press, 1986.

Sayre, Kenneth M. *Plato's Late Ontology: A Riddle Resolved.* Las Vegas, Nevada: Parmenides Press, 2005.

Sprague, Rosamond Kent. *Plato's Philosopher-King: A Study of the Theoretical Background.* Columbia, South Carolina: University of South Carolina Press, 1976.

7 Influence

Aquinas, Thomas. *On Being and Essence (De Ente et Essentia).* Translated by Armand Maurer. Toronto: Pontifical Institute of Mediaeval Studies, 1968.

Augustine. *Eighty-three Different Questions.* Fathers of the Church, vol. 70. Washington, D.C.: Catholic University Press, 1982.

Averroes. *Faith and Reason in Islam: Averroes' Exposition of Religious Arguments.* Translated by Ibrahim Y. Najjar. Oxford: Oneworld, 2001.

Avicenna. *The Metaphysics of The Healing.* Translated by Michael Marmura. Brigham Young University Press, 2005.

Plotinus. *Enneads*. Translated by A. H. Armstrong. Loeb Classical
Library. Cambridge, Mass.: Harvard University Press, 1966–88. 7
vols. See esp. 5.3, 6.1, 6.2, 6.7.

INDEX